International Crises
and the Role of Law

SUEZ
1956

International Crises
and the Role of Law

SUEZ
1956

ROBERT R. BOWIE

Published under the auspices of the
American Society of International Law

1974
Oxford University Press
New York and London

© Oxford University Press   1974
Library of Congress Catalogue Card Number: 74-16799
Printed in the United States of America

For T

FOREWORD

IF we want law and legal institutions to play larger and more effective roles in coping with international conflict, we shall need to understand more clearly the roles they now play. This book is one significant step in the search for such understanding. It is the product of a keen and experienced mind looking closely at one international crisis to learn more about the ways in which law affected—and failed to affect—decisions that were being made.

Under the auspices of the American Society of International Law, a group of us set out, individually and collectively, to learn more about the roles which law plays in the making of decisions at a time of crisis—a crisis which involves issues of war and peace. That legal considerations do play various roles in many important government decisions is clear. It is also clear that many other factors—military, political, economic, psychological, historical, cultural, social and so forth—also have effect on such decisions. Little is to be gained through argument over the comparative importance in any one decision of the different contributing elements. That law played a ten per cent role or a sixty per cent role tells us nothing about how to increase that role. What one needs to know is not *how much* did law affect a given decision, but *how*. What are the different ways in which law and legal institutions affect what happens in international affairs? This book is part of the quest for useful categories of thought to help us all to understand better how international law works and how it fails to work. It is part of the search for practical insights that may lay a foundation for measures designed to expand or strengthen the roles which law plays.

Work of the American Society of International Law in this sphere was made possible by a generous grant of the Old Dominion Foundation (a predecessor to the Andrew W. Mellon Foundation). This monograph has been commissioned and is published under the auspices of the American Society of International Law. Although the author retains full responsibility for the text, an earlier draft of the text was reviewed and discussed by a panel of members of the Society in furtherance of the project. As chairman of the panel, I would like to express our appreciation to the Foundation, to the Society, and particularly to its Executive Director, Professor Stephen M. Schwebel, for supporting and guiding this project from conception to fruition.

ROGER FISHER

Harvard Law School

PREFACE

THIS study of the Suez Crisis of 1956 seeks to explore what part international law, norms, or agencies played in the decisions and actions of the major protagonists. How did such rules, norms, or agencies influence what was done or how it was done? How were they used for legitimating political actions, for rallying support, or for imposing restraints? What role did they play in resolving the crisis?

The purpose, therefore, is not to recount the history of the crisis in detail or in all its aspects. Such accounts have already produced several very thick tomes. Yet the legal aspects cannot be treated in isolation. They were clearly only one dimension of this complex and tangled conflict, as it moved from diplomacy to force and merged with Arab–Israeli hostility. Each of the major parties —Egypt, Great Britain, France, Israel, the U.S. and the U.S.S.R.— approached the Canal issue within the context of its general policies and purposes, including rivalries in the Middle East, the Atlantic Alliance, and the Cold War.

The explicit conflict related to the control of the Canal and guarantees for its secure use, and centred on legal rights and obligations and effective means to enforce or defend them. How could the users ensure that Nasser would manage the Canal efficiently and not misuse its control to serve his political purposes? This controversy was enmeshed, however, in a wider struggle among the parties regarding influence and roles in the Middle East. In this context, the Canal dispute was an episode, a provocation, or an opportunity. The dual character of the crisis is reflected in its two phases: the first extending from the nationalization on 26 July to the end of October: and the second from the Israeli attack to the withdrawal of forces and the reopening of the Canal in April 1957. The body of the study examines the role of law in the handling of the dispute during these two phases. Its focus is mainly on the policies and actions of the United States, Great Britain and France, Egypt, and Israel. The Soviet role is treated to only a limited extent, largely for lack of data and space. The last chapter draws some conclusions regarding the role of law in this crisis.

This essay is based on published materials, especially memoirs of key participants and official documents, as well as earlier studies of the episode. My interpretations have no doubt been influenced by impressions gained at the time, when I was Assistant Secretary of State for Policy Planning and took part in certain of the decisions affecting the crisis, though not in its day-to-day handling.

In preparing this study I have had assistance and comments from many sources. I am much indebted to a series of able research assistants: William R. Brown; Michael Leigh; Michael J. McIntyre; Susan Meyer; Dominique Moisi; Stewart Reiser; Glenn E. Shealey; George Z. Singal. I have had the advantage of informed comments on the manuscript from four friends who were officials during the crisis: Herman Phleger, Francis Wilcox, Robert Amory Jr., and Chester Cooper. The study has also benefited from the suggestions of an Advisory Committee of the American Society of International Law, which commissioned it. Finally, the Harvard Center for International Affairs has provided the facilities and congenial atmosphere for the research and writing. In particular, Mrs. Dorothy Whitney, the editor of the Center, has been responsible for making the text more readable and preparing the manuscript for the press; and Miss Sally Cox, now its administrative officer, has contributed greatly to the completion of this study. For such errors of fact or judgement as remain, I am, of course, responsible.

ROBERT R. BOWIE

Center for International Affairs,
  Harvard University
    15 March, 1973

ACKNOWLEDGEMENTS

THE extracts from a letter and telegrams from Lord Avon to Dwight D. Eisenhower, quoted in *The Memoirs of Anthony Eden, part 2: Full Circle*, are reproduced by permission of the Controller of Her Majesty's Stationery Office (Crown Copyright).

The letter from Dag Hammarskjold to Dr. Fawzi, of 24 October 1956, taken from the Department of State, *United States Policy in the Middle East, September 1956–June 1957*, is reproduced by permission of the Superintendent of Documents, The United States Government Printing Office.

Four letters from Dwight D. Eisenhower to Lord Avon, taken from *The White House Years: Waging Peace 1956–1961*, copyright © 1965 by Dwight D. Eisenhower, are reprinted by permission of Doubleday and Company, Inc., and William Heinemann Ltd.

CONTENTS

CHRONOLOGY

5 January 1856	Initial Concession for the construction of the Suez Canal.
22 February 1866	Convention between Viceroy of Egypt and Suez Maritime Company.
19 August 1882	Britain moves forces into Egypt.
29 October 1888	Constantinople Convention on Suez Canal signed.
26 August 1936	Anglo-Egyptian treaty signed.
14 May 1948	Ben-Gurion proclaims establishment of Israel.
24 February 1949	Egypt–Israel armistice signed.
25 May 1950	U.S., Britain, and France issue Tripartite Declaration guaranteeing Middle East borders and barring arms race.
1 July 1951	Egypt blockades Gulf of Aqaba.
1 September 1951	Security Council calls on Egypt to end Suez restrictions on Israel.
23 July 1952	Officers' *coup* ousts Egyptian king.
1 August 1954	Israel begins secret arms purchases from France.
19 October 1954	British sign Suez base evacuation agreement with Nasser.
24 February 1955	Iraq and Turkey sign Baghdad Pact.
28 February 1955	Israel carries out the Gaza Raid.
5 April 1955	U.K. joins Baghdad Pact.
18 May 1955	Nasser initiates Soviet arms deal.
21 November 1955	Egypt, U.S., Britain begin talks in Washington on Aswan High Dam financing.
13 June 1956	Britain completes Suez base evacuation five days early.
19 July 1956	Dulles withdraws Aswan Dam offer.
26 July 1956	Nasser nationalizes Suez Canal.
1–3 August 1956	U.K., U.S., and France confer in London and agree to call London conference on Suez.

2 August 1956	U.K. initiates Anglo-French military planning for invasion of Egypt.
23 August 1956	Eighteen members of London Conference agree on Suez proposal and name Committee of five nations under Menzies (Australian Prime Minister) to 'present and explain' it to Nasser.
3–9 September 1956	Menzies Committee meets with Nasser, who rejects proposal.
12 September 1956	Eden, with U.S. and France, announces plan for setting up S.C.U.A.
15 September 1956	European pilots leave Egypt.
19–21 September 1956	Second London Conference of eighteen nations agrees to form S.C.U.A.
23 September 1956	Britain and France refer Suez dispute to U.N. Security Council.
5 October 1956	Security Council begins consideration of Suez problem.
9–12 October 1957	Security Council meets secretly, with private talks among Foreign Ministers of Britain, France, and Egypt.
13 October 1956	Security Council and Egypt accept Six Principles.
16 October 1956	Eden and Mollet meet in Paris and decide to act jointly with Israel.
22–24 October 1956	Britain, France, and Israel meet secretly at Sèvres and sign accord for collusion. Russian forces invade Budapest.
29 October 1956	Israeli forces attack Egyptian Army in Sinai.
30 October 1956	Britain and France deliver ultimatum to Israel and Egypt and veto Security Council resolutions.
31 October 1956	Anglo-French air forces attack Egyptian airfields. Security Council calls emergency meeting of General Assembly.
2 November 1956	Israeli forces occupy Gaza and Sinai. General Assembly calls for ceasefire and withdrawal.

3 November 1956	Britain and France give conditions for ceasefire. Israel accepts ceasefire, provided Egypt does the same.
4 November 1956	U.N. General Assembly adopts plan for Emergency Force. Egypt accepts ceasefire. Israeli reply is conditional.
5 November 1956	Britain and France drop paratroops at Port Said and Port Fuad; agree to cease military action when U.N.E.F. plan has been accepted by U.N. and Egypt.
6 November 1956	Anglo-French seaborne force invades Port Said. Eden and Mollet agree to ceasefire.
7 November 1956	Anglo-French troops cease fire. U.N. General Assembly agrees to set up U.N.E.F.
12 November 1956	U.N. announces Egypt has agreed to accept U.N. forces, provided Egyptian sovereignty not infringed.
15 November 1956	First contingents of U.N. force arrive in Egypt.
3 December 1956	Lloyd announces British and French will withdraw from Egypt.
7 December 1956	British House of Commons endorses withdrawal of British forces from Port Said area.
22 December 1956	British and French complete withdrawal from Egypt.
31 December 1956	Canal clearance begins under U.N. auspices.
2 February 1957	U.N. General Assembly adopts resolutions on Israeli withdrawal and U.N.E.F. role.
11 February 1957	U.S. *aide-mémoire* supports Israeli right of 'innocent passage' in Gulf of Aqaba.
20 February 1957	Eisenhower makes television speech regarding Israeli withdrawal.
1 March 1957	Israel announces withdrawal plans in U.N. General Assembly.
7–8 March 1957	Israeli troops withdrawn from Gaza Strip; replaced by U.N.E.F.
8 April 1957	Suez Canal reopens.
24 April 1957	Egypt issues declaration on Canal regime.

ABBREVIATIONS

Department of State, *Middle East*	Department of State, *United States Policy in the Middle East, September 1956–June 1957* (U.S. Government Printing Office, Washington, D.C., 1957).
Department of State, *Suez*	Department of State, *The Suez Canal Problem: July 26–September 22, 1956* (U.S. Government Printing Office, Washington, D.C., 1956).
Dep't of State Bull.	Department of State Bulletin.
Documents on International Affairs	*Documents on International Affairs 1956*, ed. Noble Frankland (Oxford University Press, London, 1959).
Eden	Anthony Eden, *The Memoirs of Anthony Eden: Full Circle* (Houghton Mifflin, Boston, 1960).
Eisenhower	Dwight D. Eisenhower, *The White House Years: Waging Peace, 1956–1961* (Doubleday, Garden City, N.Y., 1965).
H.C. Deb.	Great Britain, *Parliamentary Debates* (Commons).
H.L. Deb.	Great Britain, *Parliamentary Debates* (Lords).
Macmillan	Harold Macmillan, *Riding the Storm: 1956–1959* (Macmillan, London, 1971).
Moncrieff	Anthony Moncrieff (ed.), *Suez Ten Years After* (British Broadcasting Corporation, London, 1967).
U.N. GAOR	United Nations, General Assembly, *Official Records*.
U.N. SCOR	United Nations, Security Council, *Official Records*.

BIBLIOGRAPHICAL NOTE

THE material for this book has been drawn from published documents, general treatments of the Suez crisis, and personal memoirs or autobiographies. The most important works are cited in the notes. Since the book is not intended to be an exhaustive or original study of the event, citations have been kept to a minimum.

There are a number of general treatments of the crisis, including Herman Finer's *Dulles Over Suez: The Theory and Practice of His Diplomacy*; Kennett Love's *Suez: The Twice-Fought War*; and Terence Robertson's *Crisis: The Inside Story of the Suez Conspiracy*.

Perhaps the most useful group of sources has been the autobiographies and personal memoirs of men involved in the crisis such as Anthony Eden, Dwight D. Eisenhower, R. A. Butler, Harold Macmillan, Anthony Nutting, David Ben-Gurion, General Dayan, and General Beaufre; as well as the authorized biography of Dag Hammarskjold by Brian Urquhart; and the personal interviews of some of the major actors in Anthony Moncrieff's *Suez, Ten Years Later*.

I

THE SETTING OF THE CRISIS

NASSER provoked the Suez Crisis of 1956 by a formal decree and a fiery speech. This blending of the legal and political was typical of the course of the controversy.

1. NATIONALIZATION

His decree, published in the Official Gazette for 26 July 1956, issued Law No. 285 of 1956 'on the Nationalization of the Universal Company of the Suez Maritime Canal'. It was technical and precise. Under it, Egypt took over all assets, rights, and obligations of the Company, dissolved all its instruments for management, and created a separate Egyptian agency to operate the Canal. Shareholders of the Company were to receive compensation on the basis of the last-quoted price for the shares on the Paris Bourse on the preceding day, payable when Egypt had received *all* the assets and property of the Company (including those located abroad). Employees of the Company were required to continue working under threat of stiff penalties.[1]

Nasser sought, however, to maximize the political impact of the nationalization. He announced it in an impassioned speech in Alexandria, marking the fourth anniversary of the Egyptian Revolution. As he spoke, officials moved in dramatically to take over physical control of the Canal and Company offices.

The motives and purposes Nasser used to justify his action could not fail deeply to trouble Canal users and all states interested in the Middle East. He attacked the 'imperialists', 'colonialists', and others who had dominated and exploited Egypt in the past. The Canal, which was supposed to benefit Egypt, had become an instrument of such exploitation and domination: while Egypt had lost its Canal shares and income, the Company had become a 'state within a state' and, from 1882 on, Britain had occupied Egypt. The I.B.R.D. conditions for financing the projected Aswan Dam

[1] Department of State, *Suez*, pp. 30–2. Later Nasser offered compensation on the basis of the average price of the shares for the preceding six months.

reminded him of the earlier exploitation of the Canal concession. Now, by taking over the Canal and its control, Egypt was merely restoring its usurped rights. Although the Canal was 'a part of Egypt and belong[ed] to Egypt', Egypt was receiving only about $3 million yearly from the Canal. By nationalizing the Canal Company, Nasser said, the total revenues from the Canal—about $100 million a year or $500 million over five years—could be devoted to building the Aswan Dam. Western aid would then be unnecessary.[2]

Nasser's act of nationalization served both his external and domestic political purposes. His defiance of the West and his bold assertion of independence appealed to strong Arab and Egyptian feelings. Since the building of the Aswan Dam was at the centre of his drive for social reform and economic progress, the claim that the Canal revenues would enable Egypt itself to finance the dam was sure to be popular. It meant that Egypt could achieve its internal objectives, despite the machinations of the 'imperialists'.

2. IMPACT ON THE CANAL REGIME

Canal users had come to take for granted its availability on the basis of the existing regime. The Canal had become the vital artery for the flow of exports, imports, and shipping of many nations, and especially for Europe's access to the Middle East oil essential for its economy. Canal traffic, which had grown steadily, was expected to increase even faster in the future to meet Europe's rapidly expanding oil needs.[2a]

Prior regime of the Canal. Before nationalization the Canal regime had been composed of several elements. Since the opening of the Canal in 1869, it had been operated by the Universal Company of the Suez Maritime Canal, which had managed and maintained it efficiently and expanded it to meet growing needs. The Suez Canal Company had been formed and the Canal had been constructed on the basis of concessions by the Viceroy of Egypt

[2] Ibid., pp. 25–30.

[2a] In the four years between 1951 and 1955, total tonnage rose almost 50 per cent, exceeding 207 million tons in 1955, with more than 87 million tons moving from south to north. Some 67 million tons were Middle East oil, which provided about one-half of Europe's oil needs, with the U.K. receiving 20.5 million tons, France 12.1 million tons, Italy and the Netherlands 7.3 million each. Oil for the U.S. amounted to 8.6 million tons. Agricultural products and minerals and metals also flowed north through the Canal. The south-bound traffic included large quantities of manufactured machinery, metal products, railway equipment, etc. (D. C. Watt, *Britain and the Suez Canal* [Royal Institute of International Affairs, London, 1956], pp. 9, 13–14, 20–1).

in 1854 and 1856. With some changes, these were definitively confirmed by a Convention of 1866 made between the Viceroy and the Company and ratified by the Sultan of Turkey, the formal sovereign. The concessions were to last for ninety-nine years from the opening of the Canal, or until 1968, when the Egyptian government was to replace the Company and to acquire possession of the Canal with compensation to the Company only for equipment and moveable property.

Article 14 of the 1856 Concession declared that the Canal 'shall be open forever as neutral passage to every merchant vessel crossing from one sea to the other without any distinction, exclusion, or preference with respect to persons or nationalities', subject to payment of the tolls and compliance with the regulations of the Company. And Article 15 expressly forbade the Company to discriminate in favour of or against any vessel, company, or party.[3]

Article 16 of the Convention of 1866 provided that 'the Company being Egyptian' was to be governed by the laws and customs of Egypt except that its corporate constitution would be regulated by the French laws applicable to joint stock companies. Disputes in Egypt between the Company and private individuals of whatever nationality were to be settled in the local courts, as were any disputes between the Egyptian government and the Company.[4]

Originally, Egypt received 15 per cent of the net profits, and also acquired about 44 per cent of the shares issued by the Company. Later, its claim to profits was alienated, and its shares in the Company were sold to the British government in 1875.

The formal regime for the Canal was 'completed' by the Convention of 1888. Shortly after the Canal's opening in 1869, questions had arisen about its use by warships, especially those of belligerents during wartime. In 1870, during the Franco-German war, Egypt had allowed ships of both parties to use the Canal. In 1877, the issue had again come to the fore in the war between Russia and Turkey, the sovereign of Egypt. The United Kingdom, already heavily dependent on the Canal, declared its concern that no hostilities should occur in the canal area; Russia expressly disclaimed any intention to blockade the Canal and recognized that it should be free from attack. No incidents occurred.

This experience prompted a protracted series of discussions and meetings with a view to settling the status of the Canal by treaty.

[3] Department of State, *Suez*, p. 7.
[4] Ibid., p. 15.

The United Kingdom, which then had forces in Egypt, was not willing to accept a system for internationalizing the Canal, as some of the other powers, especially France, Germany, and Russia, urged. The outcome of a decade of negotiation was the Convention of 1888, which still governs the status of the Canal.

The Convention sought to guarantee that the Suez Canal would always be open 'in time of war as in time of peace, to every vessel of commerce or of war without distinction of flag' (Article 1). Much of the Convention was devoted to regulating the conduct of belligerents in using the Canal in wartime, which they were free to do even if Turkey was involved. By Article 9, the government of Egypt was to take all measures needed for ensuring the execution of the treaty. Turkey was to be allowed to take necessary measures to ensure the defence of Egypt (Article 10), but such measures could not interfere with free passage in the Canal (Article 11). Because of a British reservation, the Convention became effective only in 1904.[5]

The 1956 dispute brought to light one other legal document, dating from 1873. At a meeting of an international commission held in Constantinople that year, Turkey declared (and others accepted) that Suez Canal tolls and other charges or conditions of passage would not be modified without approval of the Sultan, who would act only on the basis of 'an understanding with the principal Powers interested therein'. Apparently this procedure had never actually been followed.[6]

The system in practice. In the actual regime of the Canal, the United Kingdom played the crucial role through most of the Canal's history. In 1875, it acquired 44 per cent of the Suez Company shares from Egypt, and from 1882 to 1956 it stationed troops in Egypt to protect the Canal, thus maintaining virtual control over it. From 1882 to 1914, British forces were there in theory with the consent of Turkey, of which Egypt was nominally a part. In 1914, Great Britain unilaterally declared Egypt a protectorate; and in 1922, in granting independence to Egypt, it reserved exclusive control of the defence of Egypt and protection of the Canal. By virtue of a new treaty made in 1936, the United Kingdom was to enjoy the right to keep troops in the Canal Zone for the protection of the Canal until Egypt was in a position to defend it.

British control did not affect the use of the Canal during peace-

[5] Ibid., pp. 16–20.
[6] *The Times* (London), 10 September 1956, p. 9.

time. But the situation was otherwise in wartime. During the First World War, the United Kingdom may have kept within the letter of the 1888 Convention, but it hardly conformed to its spirit. On 7 August 1914, it formally closed the Canal to German shipping on the ground that there was a risk of blockage. During the Second World War, the Convention of 1888 was virtually suspended. From the start, the Canal was closed to hostile shipping; the use of allied military vessels severely limited passage by neutral vessels; and Britain violated express provisions of Articles 4, 5, and 7 by stationing warships in the Canal, by refuelling, and by taking on and landing war materiel and troops at Canal ports and in the Canal Zone. For their part, the Axis Powers made repeated raids on the Canal. Neutral states, however, continued to respect the 1888 Convention.

After the Second World War, the role of Egypt changed. In 1948, during the Arab–Israeli fighting, it effectively closed the Canal to Israeli ships and cargo; and it maintained restrictions after the armistice of February 1949 on the grounds that belligerency continued. Egypt's method was to impose search and seizure of war contraband at the ports at either end of the Canal. It justified this action by analogy to the Allied practices in the First and Second World Wars and by Article 10 of the 1888 Convention. In 1951, Egypt rejected a call by the U.N. Security Council to reopen the Canal to Israeli shipping. When Israel again raised the issue in the Security Council in 1954, the Soviet Union vetoed action, but Egypt voluntarily relaxed its restrictions to allow goods destined for Israel to transit the Canal provided they were not carried in Israeli ships.

Then, in October 1954, in a new treaty with Egypt, Britain agreed to withdraw all its troops by June 1956; it was entitled to return them only if a power other than Israel attacked a member of the Arab League or Turkey. Article 8 of the treaty reaffirmed the guarantee of free passage through the Canal in conformity with the 1888 Convention. It also recognized both that the Canal was an integral part of Egypt and that it was of international importance.[7] In accordance with this treaty, the last British forces left Egypt in mid-June 1956.

Role of the Company. What was the role of the Canal Company in this system? Clearly, the Company did not guarantee access to the Canal in practice. While Great Britain had forces in Egypt, it

[7] Ibid., pp. 20–3.

had ultimate control of the use of the Canal, as the experience of the First and Second World Wars had shown. And in that period, Britain had at least acquiesced in Egypt's denial of the Canal to Israeli shipping. Indeed, although the Company was forbidden to discriminate among users, it was given no role in assuring compliance with the Convention of 1888. Any Canal user denied its rights under the Convention would have to look elsewhere for a remedy. Under Article 8, the 'Agents in Egypt of the Signatory Powers' were charged with seeing that the Convention was carried out. In case of any threat to the security of or free passage through the Canal, they were to meet, verify the facts, and notify the government of Egypt of the danger in order that it might take proper steps to assure 'the protection and the free use of the Canal'. This procedure was apparently never used. By Article 9, the Egyptian government had the duty to 'take the necessary measures for enforcing the execution' of the Convention.[8] The convention provided no means of remedy for a violation by Egypt.

Nevertheless, for the users, the Company's operation of the Canal was a source of confidence. As a private company it provided a buffer against potential abuses which was reassuring to world shipping. The managers, employees, and governing boards of the Company were indeed multi-national, as were its shareholders. The interests of the Company offered a good prospect that it would operate the Canal efficiently for the benefit of international shipping. Moreover, its regular practice had been to develop and expand the Canal for future needs.

This situation could not have lasted much longer, however. The Canal Company's Concession was to expire in 1968. As late as June 1956, the Egyptian government seemed to assume the Concession's continuance until 1968 but not its extension beyond that date. By the terms of the Concession, when Egypt succeeded to the Canal, the Company was not to be reimbursed for its expenditures in expanding or developing the Canal. Would the Company continue to plough back its profits to expand a facility which it would cease to operate after 1968? Actually, it had already begun setting aside substantial reserves which it had not been using to develop the Canal. Thus, before the takeover in 1956, the outlook for the Canal was uncertain. There was the imminent problem of financing expansion for future needs, as the expiration

[8] Ibid., pp. 16–20.

date approached, as well as the prospect of Egyptian control after the Concession expired.

Such concerns, which had only been looming on the horizon, suddenly became urgent with nationalization. In practical terms, would Egypt be able on short notice to marshal the skills and trained people to carry on the operation of the Canal efficiently and to assure orderly passage? If Nasser intended to divert most of the revenues to building the Aswan Dam, how could the Canal be expanded and improved for the rapidly growing traffic? Would not the takeover result in much higher tolls, designed to extract maximum revenues?

3. THE GENERAL POLITICAL CONTEXT

By itself, the controversy over the regime for the Canal might have been settled peacefully in accordance with the U.N. Charter. But that dispute was enmeshed in more basic conflicts over influence and roles in the region and beyond, which could not be resolved by compromise. Those most concerned, especially Britain and France, saw the Canal dispute as a symbol and expression of these clashes in wider aims. For Nasser also, the nationalization was not an isolated action. He meant it as an episode in the political struggle in the region, as his speech showed. And the other protagonists so construed it.

Nasser had emerged as the central figure in Middle East politics after the officers' *coup* overthrew King Farouk in 1952. He seemed bent on being the leader not only of Egypt but of the region, and on exploiting its rivalries, frustrations, and aspirations to this end. Hence the obvious questions: how might Nasser try to utilize the Canal to further his foreign policy? How would his defiant gesture affect his own prestige and influence and those of others? What should be done?

These various conflicts in interests and aims interacted to form a tangled web of frictions and tensions which grew out of three distinct sources.

Local nationalism. A major source of conflict was the tension between local nationalism and Western influence, especially British. British interests in the Middle East were extensive and had deep roots, going back nearly a century. Concern for the Canal as the critical link with the Empire east of Suez had prompted Disraeli's purchase of 44 per cent of the shares in 1875, and the maintenance of British forces in Egypt from 1882 to 1956. After the First

World War and the collapse of the Ottoman Empire, Britain (and to a lesser extent, France) was predominant in the region, and it developed ties with many of the local countries and rulers. The U.K. had held the Palestine Mandate until the creation of Israel. In the Second World War, Britain virtually alone had defended the strategic Suez Canal region from the powerful Nazi thrust. After Indian independence, British interests in the Middle East, with its vast oil reserves, took on greater strategic, economic, commercial, and emotional significance. The Suez base was seen as the pivot of strategic flexibility in the Eastern Mediterranean and the means of guaranteeing the Canal.

After the Second World War, local nationalisms began to contest these historic positions founded on strategic needs or interests in oil or commerce. In 1951, Iran had nationalized the vast Abadan refinery of the Anglo-Iranian Oil Company. And in October 1951, before the officers' *coup*, Egypt had unilaterally abrogated the Anglo-Egyptian Treaty covering the Suez Canal base and had rejected a Western plan for a Middle East Defence Organization. The U.K. (with some U.S. support) had sought to link the supply of new weapons and revision of the Anglo-Egyptian Treaty to Egypt's taking part in a regional security pact.

Egypt's leaders consistently rejected these proposals. For them, an integrated defence force or even a joint command would only perpetuate Western dominance, given the extreme disparity in power and resources. In their view, the Arabs themselves should assume the task of defence, with the West supplying arms, and with the Suez base kept in standby condition for use only in case of hostilities, with no foreign forces stationed there permanently. The 1954 Anglo-Egyptian Treaty was a compromise, with the U.K. committed to withdrawing its forces by mid 1956, while being entitled to maintain the Suez base in standby condition by civilian contractors, and to use it (until 1961) in case of attack on the region by an aggressor other than Israel. Nasser's approval of the treaty led to an attempt on his life by the Moslem Brotherhood. The U.S. promptly granted Egypt $40 million in economic aid but delayed on supplying arms.

Any hope for better relations was quickly undermined by the defence issue. In essence, Nasser discounted the Soviet threat and considered Western dominance the greater danger. Consequently, his ire was aroused by the Baghdad Pact, signed by Turkey and Iraq in February 1955 and quickly joined by Britain, which had promoted it. Pakistan followed in September and Iran in November. Although the U.S. co-operated, it did not join. This pact hurt Nasser in two ways. First of all, it bolstered Anglo-American influence in the Middle East despite Egypt's opposition. Secondly, it strengthened Iran in its rivalry with Egypt for leadership within the Arab League, where Egypt had been predominant. Nasser denounced the pact as a neo-colonial threat to Arab independence. To recoup, he embraced 'active neutralism', starting with the Afro-Asian Conference at Bandung in April 1955, and cultivated contacts with Chou En-Lai, Tito, Sukarno, and Nehru. But if these contacts increased his standing at home and in the Arab world, they helped little in his contest with the West.

Arab–Israeli Hostility. A second source of tension was the Arab–Israeli conflict. Egypt's relations with Israel had of course been unfriendly since the hostilities and armistice following Israel's creation in 1948. Like other Arab states, Egypt denied Israel's legitimacy and demanded its surrender of considerable territory and restitution for the Palestinian refugees; but from time to time, Egyptian officials expressed more moderate views. The million Arab refugees, uprooted by Israel's formation and living in squalid camps, produced tension and instability.

Moreover, this conflict made arms supply another obstacle in Western relations with Egypt. Israel's defeat of the Egyptian army was one factor in the 1952 *coup d'état* of Nasser and his colleagues. Having suffered the humiliation of that defeat, they wanted to acquire modern arms and to rebuild the Egyptian army. And Israel was single-minded in the pursuit of its security and the effort to compel the Arabs to accept its presence. By the Tripartite Declaration of 1950, the U.S., U.K., and France had undertaken to regulate the arms flow to the area and preserve the armistice. For Israel, each increase in Egypt's power or regional influence was viewed as a danger to its own security. Hence the Israelis tried to prevent U.S. arms transfers to Egypt while seeking both arms and a bilateral defence commitment from the United States. But Nasser objected to any conditions related to such arms as infringing his country's independence.

For a year before February 1955, while Ben-Gurion was temporarily retired, Moshe Sharett, Prime Minister of Israel, followed a moderate course designed to reduce hostility and tension, which Nasser also claimed to desire, despite border incidents and provocative rhetoric. During this phase, however, Israel's security seemed to be impaired by several factors: Eisenhower's shift to greater impartiality, the 1954 British agreement to leave the Suez base, and the Baghdad Pact. Consequently, Israel wanted a firmer Western commitment to its security than the 1950 Tripartite Declaration.

February 1955 was a watershed in Israeli–Egyptian relations. David Ben-Gurion returned to the Cabinet (first as Defence Minister). Together with General Moshe Dayan, his policy was to coerce the Arabs into settling on Israel's terms. In February, Israel launched an unusually destructive reprisal on Egyptian forces in the Gaza Strip. That raid put Egypt and Israel on a collision course. Its consequences were inexorable: Nasser's decision to mount 'fedayeen' guerrilla-type reprisals; the succession of raids and reprisals; the expanding arms race; and, finally, the Sinai war. Reacting to the raid, Nasser placed new restrictions on foreign-flag vessels entering the Gulf of Aqaba for the Port of Eilat, which Israel had been developing to handle more traffic.

For Ben-Gurion, Nasser became the primary target. In October 1955, he directed Dayan to prepare plans for a Sinai military operation—one prime objective was to break the blockade of the Gulf of Aqaba 'within one year'. In June 1956 he forced Sharett out of the Cabinet because he was likely to oppose offensive war. But Ben-Gurion assured the Knesset then that he would never engage in any military conflict which would entail fighting against Western forces.[9] As a result of the Suez Crisis, he was able to launch his attack in October 1956 in co-operation with French and British forces, thus meeting his condition.

Soviet entry. The U.S.S.R. had been interested for some time in extending its influence in the Middle East. The Baghdad Pact, promoted by Britain, had been designed in part as a counterweight to bolster the security and confidence in the region against the potential threat of Soviet power. It was the Gaza Raid of February 1955 that opened the way for Soviet entry into the area. Nasser had been seeking arms from the West for some time with very limited success. After the Gaza Raid, he was under great pressure to obtain Western armaments to offset Israeli strength. He would still have preferred to acquire them from the West; after approaching the Soviet Ambassador in May, he virtually

[9] Michael Bar-Zohar, *Ben-Gurion: The Armed Prophet* (Prentice Hall, New York, 1968), pp. 192–4; Kennet Love, *Suez: The Twice-Fought War* (McGraw-Hill, New York, 1969), pp. 123–4.

invited the U.S. to provide an alternative. But, failing in that attempt, he completed arangements before September to obtain Soviet arms through Czechoslovakia.

Israel saw this deal as a further threat, especially because the U.S. and U.K. had not been able to prevent it. Conversely, Nasser appeared more relaxed. He stated publicly that war over access to Aqaba depended on the Israelis, and that he believed the Soviet arms would dissuade Israel from attacking Egypt. In addition, the arrival of the U.S.S.R. on the Middle East stage freed Egypt from a major constraint in its relations with the West, for it removed the contradiction inherent in attempting to reduce Western influence in the area while looking to the Western powers for arms.

The reaction of the United States and its Western partners was probably milder than Nasser expected. The U.S. attempted to convince him of the advantages of continued association with the West, hoping thereby to limit the Soviet arms deal to this single transaction. Britain and France permitted small shipments of arms to Egypt, and the British continued the withdrawal of troops from Suez well ahead of schedule. Moreover, in December 1955 the United States and Britain, together with the International Bank for Reconstruction and Development (I.B.R.D.), offered to help finance Egypt's Aswan Dam, a $1·3 billion project, requiring from twelve to fifteen years for completion. The proposals contemplated initial loans and grants of $56 million from the U.S., $14 million from the U.K., and $200 million from the I.B.R.D. to cover foreign exchange costs; some $800 million or more was to come from Egyptian resources. Negotiations dragged on for months, with Nasser objecting strenuously to the fiscal safeguards requested by the I.B.R.D.

Prelude to the Suez nationalization. The Aswan offer did nothing to moderate Nasser's attitude towards continued Western influence in the Middle East. His success in obtaining Soviet arms while eliciting Western support for Egypt's development greatly enhanced his prestige and influence in the Arab countries, which he used to carry on his active policy. He continued to attack the Baghdad Pact. To counter it, Egypt concluded bilateral defence arrangements with Syria, Saudi Arabia, and Yemen; these states made an offer to Jordan to replace the British subsidy, but King Hussein politely declined. Nasser prevailed, however, in his struggle to keep Jordan from joining the Western Alliance. Then on 1 March 1956, Hussein dismissed General Glubb, a British subject who for twenty-five years had headed Jordan's Arab Legion. This shattering blow to British standing was widely credited to Nasser's influence, whether or not he had actually promoted it. In addition, Egypt continued its support for the Algerian rebels in defiance of French threats and protests. Clearly, Egypt was not prepared to modify its regional purposes, even in exchange for the West's support for the Aswan Dam.

These activities chilled the U.S. and British interest in financing the dam, especially in view of Nasser's attitude in negotiating with I.B.R.D. Furthermore, Congress was hostile to such support for various reasons, and Egypt's heavy commitments for Soviet arms raised doubts about its capacity to provide the substantial domestic resources required to complete the dam. Accordingly, in mid-July the U.S. decided not to go forward with the project and so advised the British, who apparently had reached a similar conclusion about the same time.[10]

On 19 July 1956, Secretary John Foster Dulles notified the Egyptians of the U.S. decision and issued a press communiqué citing as reasons that recent 'developments ... had not been favourable to the success of the project' and that 'the ability of Egypt to devote adequate resources to assure the project's success has become more uncertain than at the time the offer was made'.[11] The U.K. and the I.B.R.D. followed suit.

Nasser, who was just finishing a meeting at Brioni with Tito and Nehru, took offence at the manner of the withdrawal. As a charismatic leader, he needed a bold, defiant gesture to rebuff the West. Agitating the Israelis was too risky; Egyptian forces had suffered appreciable losses in five serious incidents with Israel during 1955.[12] He had already done what he could to undermine the Baghdad Pact. He had driven the British out of the Suez base. None of these issues afforded Nasser an opportunity for a dramatic stroke. Seizure of the Canal Company, on the other hand, was an attractive possibility. It could be done by Egyptians within Egyptian territory. With all British troops gone, there would be no outsiders to block such a move. Nationalization would also serve the two basic Egyptian purposes—removal of limitations on its

[10] R. A. Butler, *The Art of the Possible: The Memoirs of Lord Butler* (Hamish Hamilton, London, 1971), pp. 185–6.

[11] Press relase of 19 July 1956, in Eisenhower, p. 663.

[12] Keith Wheelock, *Nasser's New Egypt: A Critical Analysis* (Praeger, New York, 1960), p. 223.

sovereignty, and the undercutting of Western influence in the Middle East. The Canal Concession stood as the last vestige of Egypt's subordination to the West; its termination had great appeal.

Accordingly, on 23 July, Nasser decided to nationalize the Canal Company, largely in retaliation for the refusal of the Aswan offer. The idea may not have been entirely new. In September 1954, the press had reported that the Egyptian government had named a committee to prepare for a smooth transition when the Suez Concession expired in 1968, and since November 1954, Mahmoud Younes, an Egyptian marine engineer, had, on Nasser's instructions, been secretly studying the administration, planning, and operations of the Company.[13] Hence, it was feasible to organize and execute the takeover by 26 July.

None of the Western states anticipated the nationalization on 26 July. Their decisions about how to respond were greatly influenced by the political situation in the Middle East as well as by their dependence on the Canal.

[13] Nasser interview in Moncrieff, pp. 42–3; Terence Robertson, *Crisis: The Inside Story of the Suez Conspiracy* (Atheneum, New York, 1965), p. 6.

II

POSITIONS OF THE PARTIES

DESPITE the deeper conflicts, the Suez Crisis was notable for the extent to which the parties felt impelled to frame the issues and to justify their actions or claims in terms of legal rights and obligations.[1] Their purposes in doing so were varied: to attack, to defend, to legitimate, to constrain, to dissemble, to rally support. Clearly, law did not necessarily determine decisions and actions, but it influenced and shaped them in many ways.

In legal terms, the dispute revolved around the right to nationalize the Suez Canal Company, the proper interpretation of the Convention of 1888, and the duties and constraints under the U.N. Charter. The differences among the parties did not relate primarily to the principles which should govern the use and operation of the Suez Canal. Nasser asserted that in managing the Canal, Egypt would be guided by essentially the same criteria as those which the users considered necessary for its reliability and future adequacy.

Strictly defined, the Canal controversy was about how these principles should be guaranteed and enforced. In essence, Egypt contended that its undertakings by treaty and declaration were sufficient assurance that it would operate the Canal in conformity with these principles. In general, the users, who were not satisfied to rely solely on Nasser's good faith, sought to obtain other safeguards against abuse of control. A more secure system might have taken various forms. One might have been the operation of the Canal by an international agency instead of Egypt, as proposed by eighteen major users at the London Conference (see Chapter III). Or, safeguards might have been provided by more limited arrangements which left the operation of the Canal in Egypt's hands but imposed constraints on its freedom of action.

This way of posing the issue, however, conceals a more basic

---

[1] This chapter focuses mainly on the positions of Egypt, the U.K. and U.S., and to a lesser extent, France. The Israeli position is discussed in relation to the use of force (Chapter IV). The Soviet position is not separately treated but is referred to at appropriate places.

cleavage among the major parties, which was a key to the course of the conflict. The British and French saw the dispute in wider, more political terms: they were convinced that Nasser menaced their basic positions in the Middle East, and that undermining him was essential for the protection of their wider interests, as well as for the future reliability of the Canal. They, therefore, wanted to handle the Canal dispute so as to humiliate Nasser or to create a pretext for the use of force to unseat him. The United States, however, was firmly committed to solving the Suez Crisis by peaceful means—by mobilizing pressure to induce Nasser to accept institutional guarantees of some kind for the secure use and future development of the Canal.

In consequence, the first phase of the crisis was, among other things, a disguised struggle between the U.S. and the U.K. (and France) over the handling of the problem. In the second phase, these deep-seated divergences broke into the open with the Anglo-French resort to force and the U.S. reaction to it. Thus, the course of the Suez Crisis was shaped as much, or more, by this conflict of purposes among the Western nations as by Nasser's actions.

1. THE EGYPTIAN POSITION

In taking over the Canal Company and the Canal, Nasser was obviously inspired by political motives: he wanted to retaliate for the Western refusal to finance the Aswan Dam and to provide an alternative source of financing; to demonstrate Egypt's independence; and to exploit nationalism and xenophobia at home and in the Middle East as a whole. For these purposes, the decision to nationalize and the speech announcing it were intentionally provocative, truculent, and defiant.

Having garnered the political benefits of his speech and action, Nasser at once began bolstering his defensive position against foreign opponents on both the practical and the legal planes. The day after his speech, Abu Nosseir, the Commerce Minister, played down the vengeful aspects of nationalization and attributed the act to the Company's failure to meet its obligations under the Concession. On 28 July, Nasser himself pledged that Egypt would not hamper traffic, and a spokesman said that tolls would not be raised. On 31 July, an official press handout, attributed to Nasser, declared that nationalization would in no way affect Egypt's determination to meet its international obligations. A few days later, Nasser's chief aide, Ali Sabri, rebutted the contention that navigation was being threatened by the change in the Company's status.[1a] Most important of all, traffic continued to move through the Canal without interruption and at normal volumes.

In the ensuing crisis, Nasser promptly sought to stake out a solid legal foundation for his position on all the major issues. In doing so, he clearly had the benefit of able legal advice, including a legal study of the Canal regime and the related issues which had been prepared in 1951 by Dr. Moustapha el-Hefnaoui.[2] Nasser stated his legal position when he refused the invitation to the London Conference on 12 August 1956, and he restated it in his letter of 9 September to Sir Robert Menzies rejecting the Eighteen-Power proposals (see Chapter III).

Nasser did not take issue with the basic criteria which the eighteen user countries had prescribed for a solution: that it must respect the sovereign rights of Egypt, safeguard freedom of passage through the Canal in accordance with the Convention of 1888, respect Egypt's right of ownership, and assure efficient and dependable operation, maintenance, and development of the Canal. In the letter to Menzies, Nasser stated that Egyptian policy was to assure:

(a) the freedom of passage through the Suez Canal and its secure use without discrimination;
(b) the development of the Suez Canal to meet the future requirements of navigation;
(c) the establishment of just and equitable tolls and charges; and
(d) technical efficiency of the Suez Canal.[3]

Nationalization. Under international law, Nasser claimed, Egypt was entitled to nationalize the Suez Canal Company. According to Article 16 of the 1866 agreement between Egypt and the Company, the Company was Egyptian and was subject to the laws and customs of Egypt. The Convention of 1888 had not changed the status of the Canal Company; its provisions were not to affect the sovereign rights of Egypt (Article 16). Nor was the Convention limited to the life of the Concession to the Company (Article 14). Nationalizing the Company had only accelerated the expiration of the Concession by twelve years.

[1a] Keith Wheelock, *Nasser's New Egypt: A Critical Analysis*, p. 233; Department of State, *Suez*, pp. 25–32; D. C. Watt, *Britain and the Suez Canal*, p. 25.

[2] Moustapha el-Hefnaoui, *Les problèmes contemporains posés par le Canal de Suez* (Imprimerie Guillemot et de Lamothe, Paris, 1951).

[3] Suez Committee Document SC/D/33, in Department of State, *Suez*, pp. 317–22 (quotation from 321–2).

Convention of 1888. Nasser asserted that the Convention remained in effect and was binding on Egypt, which would conform to its terms. The situation was just as it would have been if the Concession had expired in due course. The carrying out of that Convention, he argued, had always depended on Egypt and not on the Company, which had never taken any measures to assure freedom of passage through the Canal. Egypt had in no way interfered with passage through the Canal after the takeover and, indeed, had put through the Canal a volume of traffic as great as or greater than in the past. The barring of Israeli shipping, Nasser said, was compatible with the Convention in view of the continued belligerency and the British wartime practice.

Further guarantees. Nasser stated on both 12 August and 9 September that he was willing, with the other signatories of the Convention of 1888, to sponsor a conference of all users to review and reaffirm that Convention and to consider further agreements to guarantee freedom of passage through the Canal. The future of the Canal, he asserted, depended on genuine co-operation between the users and Egypt, of which the Canal was an integral part. An international agency to operate it would constitute a form of 'collective colonialism'; in practice, such an agency would only create friction within Egypt and impede the close co-operation that was essential.

U.N. Charter. Finally, Nasser appealed to the U.N. Charter, insisting on the obligation to reach a peaceful solution of the Crisis and objecting to Western measures to exert economic pressures on Egypt and also to mobilize military force. He contrasted these actions, which he said violated the spirit and letter of the Charter, with his own readiness to negotiate a peaceful solution in conformity with its principles and purposes.

Ten years later, Nasser explained his basic calculation. He had expected the nationalizing of the Canal Company to produce a loud Western outcry, but the violence of the British reaction had surprised him. Even so, he had examined the British military situation before acting and had concluded that Britain would require several months to organize any military response. In that period, he had expected to be able to work out a solution by negotiation.[4]

[4] Nasser interview in Moncrieff, p. 44.

2. THE BRITISH POSITION

The British were profoundly shocked by Nasser's action. For the Prime Minister, Eden, and his Cabinet, it appeared to pose the gravest threat to vital British interests. The situation, Eden believed, was 'certainly the most hazardous that our country has known since 1940'.[5] This conviction, shared by his key colleagues, underlay British decisions and actions during the crisis. Indeed, the basic U.K. appraisal and policy were largely settled in the first days after the nationalization.

Appraisal. Concern about the Canal alone did not explain the British reaction. The Canal was, of course, important to the United Kingdom. Its ships were the largest users of the Canal, carrying both imports and exports in large volume; and from 60 to 70 per cent of the oil required for the British economy came through the Canal from the Middle East, with the amount steadily rising. If the Canal were mismanaged, or not expanded for future needs, or used for pressure, Britain would suffer first and most. Nasser, said Eden, could not be allowed 'to have his thumb on our windpipe'.[6]

Yet, as Eden and his Cabinet perceived the situation, the seizure imperilled much more than the Canal. At stake was the whole British position in the Middle East. If unchecked, Nasser would exploit Arab nationalism to dominate the region, including the sources of Middle Eastern oil which had become the lifeblood of the British and European economies. Nasser's action and speech were only the final proof that the West could not compromise with him.

This deep distrust of Nasser and of his purposes had been building up gradually for several years. It had been fostered by the series of frictions and setbacks in the Middle East: the 1954 Suez base negotiations, the Baghdad Pact, the Arab–Israeli antagonism, the Soviet arms deal, the dismissal of Glubb, and the Aswan Dam project. Over and over, the cause of the problems, or at least a major complicating factor, was Nasser, who missed no chance to undercut British influence or interests. Thus, for Eden, both as Foreign Secretary from 1952 and then as Prime Minister from April 1955, the region and, in particular, Nasser, were a constant source of trouble.

[5] Eden, p. 506.
[6] Ibid., p. 474.

To add to his frustrations, Eden also had to contend with criticism of his course from the Suez Group of Tories, the Tory press, and even Churchill, as well as with the reluctance of Eisenhower and Dulles to put pressure on the Egyptians. As time went on, comments began to be voiced in the press and the party about 'indecision' and 'appeasement' of Britain's enemies. The base agreement, the mild response to Glubb's dismissal, the limited support for Israel, and the Aswan offer could be exploited to revive memories of Munich. Eden, who was especially sensitive to such criticism after becoming Prime Minister, felt pressed to vindicate his own image of himself as an anti-appeaser.

For Eden the abrupt dismissal of General Glubb by King Hussein on 1 March 1956 had been the last straw; ignoring Hussein's own reasons for the step, Eden assumed that Nasser had engineered it. Since Eden could not afford to break with Hussein, his pent-up frustration was primarily focused on Nasser. Thenceforth, according to Anthony Nutting, Eden never uttered Nasser's name without emotion. British security, safeguarding the Canal, building the Baghdad Pact, protecting Israel—all these aims coalesced towards a single goal: to destroy Nasser.

Eden was quite explicit about his objective more than four months before the Suez Crisis. After reading a Foreign Office analysis of Britain's options, the Prime Minister exploded to Nutting: 'But what's all this nonsense about isolating Nasser or "neutralising" him, as you call it? I want him destroyed, can't you understand? I want him removed . . .' When it was pointed out that Nasser's removal would lead to anarchy in Egypt, his reply was equally direct: 'But I don't want an alternative. . . . And I don't give a damn if there's anarchy and chaos in Egypt.'[7]

The sudden nationalization only confirmed and reinforced Eden's distrust and hostility. Nasser was not only flouting international agreements; he was also challenging Britain's historic role and wider interests. Moreover, this appraisal of Nasser's actions was not confined to Eden and his Cabinet. On the contrary, it was generally shared in Britain. The press condemned Nasser almost with one voice. On 1 August, for example, *The Times* (London) said editorially:

If Nasser is allowed to get away with his *coup* all the British and other Western interests in the Middle East will crumble. It is a 'turning point'

[7] Anthony Nutting, *No End of a Lesson: The Story of Suez* (Clarkson N. Potter, 1967), pp. 31, 34, 35.

in history like Hitler's march into the Rhineland or Stalin's takeover of Czechoslovakia. Quibbling over whether or not he was 'legally entitled' to make the grab will delight the finicky and comfort the faint-hearted, but entirely misses the real issues.[8]

The virtual unanimity of such judgements was shown by the eloquent speech of Hugh Gaitskell, Leader of the Labour Opposition, in the House of Commons on 2 August. The 1888 Convention was not an adequate safeguard against abuse of unilateral Egyptian control, Gaitskell declared. The barring of Israeli shipping from the Canal, in defiance of the 1951 Security Council resolution, was hardly reassuring; and confidence was inevitably shaken by the way nationalization had been carried out and justified: 'It was done suddenly, without negotiation, without discussion, by force, and ... on the excuse that this was the way to finance the Aswan Dam project.' But even more troubling were the wider implications:

We cannot forget that Colonel Nasser has repeatedly boasted of his intention to create an Arab empire from the Atlantic to the Persian Gulf.... This episode must be recognized as part of the struggle for the mastery of the Middle East.... If Colonel Nasser's prestige is put up sufficiently and ours is put down, the effects of that in that part of the world will be that our friends desert us because they think we are lost, and go over to Egypt.
I have no doubt myself that the reason why Colonel Nasser acted in the way that he did, aggressively, brusquely, suddenly, was precisely because he wanted to raise his prestige in the rest of the Middle East....
It is all very familiar. It is exactly the same as we encountered from Mussolini and Hitler in those years before the war. We must not underestimate the danger of the effect which this may have on the other Arab States.[9]

This analogy with Hitler or Mussolini, and with Munich, however far-fetched as applied to Nasser, was widely invoked at the time of the Suez Crisis by Eden and his Cabinet colleagues, the Tory Right and leading newspapers, and initially by the Labour Front Bench. Harold Macmillan, then Chancellor of the Exchequer,

[8] Eden, p. 491.
[9] Great Britain, H.C. Deb., vol. 557, col. 1609–17, 2 Aug. 1956, in *The Commonwealth and Suez, a Documentary Survey*, ed. James Eayrs (Oxford University Press, London, 1964), pp. 33–7.

publicized it repeatedly, as did Guy Mollet, then French Premier.[10]

Eden set out the appraisal and attitude of the Cabinet forcefully in a cable to President Eisenhower on 27 July. In it he rehearsed the concrete dangers inherent in Nasser's action—the threat to the influence of the United Kingdom and the United States in the Middle East, the jeopardy for Western Europe's oil supplies, and the diversion of Canal revenues to Egypt's internal purposes. But the Prime Minister was quite clear that these specific problems paled before the enormity of 'the longer term outlook'.

We should not allow ourselves to become involved in legal quibbles about the rights of the Egyptian Government to nationalize what is technically an Egyptian company, or in financial arguments about their capacity to pay the compensation which they have offered. I feel sure that we should take issue with them on the broader international grounds.[11]

Basic policy. On this analysis, the Cabinet concluded that Nasser must not be allowed 'to get away with' the seizure of control of the Canal. The object must be 'to undo' Nasser's action and put the Canal firmly in international custody. According to Eden, the Cabinet decided that (1) 'our essential interests in this area must be safeguarded, if necessary, by military action'; (2) 'failure to keep the canal international would inevitably lead to the loss one by one of all our interests and assets in the Middle East'; (3) 'even if Her Majesty's government had to act alone they could not stop short of using force to protect their position'; and (4) the Chiefs of State should prepare 'a plan and time-table for an operation designed to occupy and secure the canal, should other methods fail' (as seemed likely).[12]

This course really combined two aims, as Lord Butler pointed out. One was to prevent unilateral Egyptian control, with the risk of its abuse. (For this, international operation might be the most secure means, but not the sole one.) The other aim, shared by some of the Cabinet, and based on the Munich analogy, was 'to reduce the stature of the megalomaniacal dictator at an early stage'. Butler thought that many Cabinet members 'were muddled by this duality of purpose'.[13] But Eden was cer-

---

[10] Pineau interview in Moncrieff, pp. 35–6; Macmillan, pp. 100, 111, 155–6; Eden, pp. 430–1; R. A. Butler, *The Art of the Possible: The Memoirs of Lord Butler*, pp. 188–9.

[11] Eden, pp. 476–7.   [12] Ibid., pp. 474–5.
[13] Butler, pp. 188–9.

tainly clear about the relation of the two aims. If Nasser were compelled to 'undo' the nationalization and turn over the Canal to international control, he would be discredited and deflated. He would hardly do so, therefore, unless coerced by force—which might well result in unseating him. Thus, the Canal dispute could be the instrument for humiliating or getting rid of Nasser, if the demand for international control were rigidly maintained. The same view was doubtless held by Macmillan, Lord Salisbury, and probably others of the seven-man inner group of the Cabinet which managed the crisis.

Apparently, the Cabinet considered whether to send an Anglo-French ultimatum at once to Nasser—or to await speedy meeting of the major maritime powers before sending a joint demand. On the question whether the U.K. and France should have forcibly reoccupied the Canal at once, Eden later gave two answers. First, as U.N. members, they were obliged initially to seek redress by peaceful means, including the Security Council, even though the Soviet veto made action unlikely. Second, six weeks or more would have been required to prepare the logistics for an assault from Malta.[14]

From the start, Eden indicated to President Eisenhower that Britain was contemplating force. In his cable of 27 July, Eden informed the President: 'My colleagues and I are convinced that we must be ready, in the last resort, to use force to bring Nasser to his senses. For our part we are prepared to do so. I have this morning instructed our Chiefs of Staff to prepare a military plan accordingly.'[15] On 29 July, this message was reinforced when Macmillan confided to Robert Murphy, Eisenhower's special envoy, his government's resolve to wrest the Canal from Nasser by force. Publicly, Eden announced 'certain precautionary measures of a military nature', including the recall of several classes of reserves and a strategic build-up in the Eastern Mediterranean. This gratified the Suez Group of Tories since reserves could not be kept mobilized indefinitely or demobilized without weakening Britain's bargaining position.

In fact, as the Cabinet knew, any resort to force would require at least six weeks to organize and would entail grave risks without U.S. backing or at least acquiescence. An attack on Egypt involved serious prospects that Canal traffic would be blocked by sinkings or guerrilla action and that pipelines would be cut in other Arab

14 Eden, pp. 482–3, 478–9.   15 Ibid., p. 477.

states. Europe would suffer severe shortages of oil, which could be made up only with help from the U.S. Similarly, the U.K. needed to count on the U.S. to deter the U.S.S.R. from intervening in case of an attack on Egypt. Eden and his colleagues doubtless hoped that the U.S. might be induced to acquiesce in the use of force and even assist in dealing with potential oil shortages and the Soviet threat, if the U.K. and France purported to have exhausted peaceful means for solving the crisis.

Although Eden did not want to 'quibble' over legalities, he quickly recognized that it was essential to lay a solid foundation to justify ultimate use of force, if necessary, and to obtain the support of public opinion. Consequently, the legal aspects could not be ignored, even though they were not controlling. The Prime Minister and the Foreign Secretary, therefore, elaborated to the House of Commons, to President Eisenhower, and for history, the magnitude of Nasser's breach of international law. In a speech to the House on 2 August, Eden rested his case upon: (1) the Suez Canal Company's Concession Agreements, and their frequent and recent endorsements by the Egyptian Government; and (2) the 1888 Convention, upheld in the Anglo-Egyptian Agreement of 1954. Eden relied on the international character of the Canal Company, which, 'although ... registered in Egypt, is of course an international organization ...' Accordingly, the normal right of a state to nationalize could not properly be exercised to take over such an international public utility.[16] This contention was the key to Britain's legal interpretation. It took direct issue with Nasser's legal claim that 'we only nationalized an Egyptian limited liability company, and by so doing we exercised a right which stems from the very core of Egyptian sovereignty'.[17]

While it might seem logically to follow that the Suez Canal should be restored to the Company, the remedy claimed was for its transfer to international control. The reasons were practical: first, a demand to reinstate the private Company would have alienated many newer nations, much more than would the creation of an international agency; for they would not have accepted any restriction on the general right to nationalize. Second, since the conces-

[16] Great Britain, H.C. Deb., vol. 557, col. 1602–8, 2 Aug. 1956, in *Documents on International Affairs*, pp. 125–7. Some M.P.s also cited Nasser's disregard of the 1951 Security Council Resolution requiring freedom for Israeli commerce in the Canal.

[17] Nasser's Cairo speech in Department of State, *Suez*, pp. 25–30.

sion of the Company had only twelve years left to run, the same issue of Egyptian control would arise again when the legal case against it would be much weaker.

The argument that the takeover was unlawful did not necessarily establish the right to resort to force to remedy it. That point was left vague at this stage. On both aspects of his legal position, however, Eden had the support of the Lord Chancellor, who attended the Cabinet meeting on 26 July. Later he wrote:

From the first I thought that it was wrong in international law to end unilaterally and by threat of force the international control of an international waterway. The Suez Canal Company had been treated as an international entity and was the basis of the international control. I further took the view that to destroy this basis and end international control by force was forcible aggression against a territory marked with an international character which, if the other procedures of the Charter produced no result, could be decided by force under Article 51 of the Charter of the United Nations. For the last proposition I must admit that I could not get any support from international lawyers, except from Professor Arthur Goodhart.[18]

Certainly the Lord Chancellor's proposition had no support from Lord McNair, a former President of the International Court of Justice. Speaking in the House of Lords on 12 September, he stressed the international character of the Company and the Canal, concluding that the users, and especially Great Britain, were 'fully justified to press for the negotiation of some kind of international system or guarantee to secure the uninterrupted and efficient use of this "great international waterway".' But just as emphatically he was 'unable to see the legal justification of the threat or use of armed force by Great Britain against Egypt in order to impose a solution of this dispute'.[19]

The Labour Party also did not support any use of force outside the U.N. framework. Even in his speech of 2 August, already quoted, which endorsed the main tenets of the government's revealed position, the Leader of the Opposition warned against considering hypothetical situations in which force *might* be necessary. The British record for respect of international law was impeccable: 'We must not, therefore, allow ourselves to get into a position where we might be denounced by the Security Council as

[18] David P. M. Fyfe, *Political Adventure: The Memoirs of the Earl of Kilmuir* (Weidenfeld and Nicolson, London, 1964), p. 268.
[19] Great Britain, H.L. Deb., vol. 199, col. 657–63, 12 Sept. 1956.

aggressors, or where the majority of the Assembly were against us.'[20] In practice, Gaitskell's opposition to the use of force outside the U.N. was tantamount to 'no force under any circumstances', given the composition of the U.N. Assembly and Security Council. The Opposition's stance was all the more galling to Eden because it corresponded to the U.S. position. Labour Party spokesmen took up those pronouncements of the Secretary of State which were most resented by the British government; by mid-September, the Labour Party and the Secretary of State were equally adamant in their renunciations of force.

After the first shock wore off, divergences became more apparent. Gaitskell, speaking for the Labour Party, demurred at Eden's extreme diagnosis. The seeming bi-partisan solidarity in Parliament faded as the specific questions were confronted—the validity of nationalization in international law, the status of the Canal Company, the ability of the Egyptians to run the Canal, the propriety of unilateral intervention, the role of the United Nations, and the coherence of the Western Alliance.

Finally, Eden felt a personal antipathy for Gaitskell and for Dulles. This accentuated his difficulties in working with these men and heightened his sense of betrayal. Of Gaitskell, Eden noted a unique 'cast of mind and approach to problems' which precluded the kind of rapport he felt he had with Attlee—'We never seemed able to get on terms.' The Prime Minister characterized Dulles as 'a preacher in the world of politics ... [with] little regard for the consequence of his words'.[21]

The divergences went far deeper than matters of personality, however. They sprang from basic cleavages in appraisals, interests, and purposes. In essence, Eden and his colleagues were committed to Nasser's downfall, which could not be achieved by a peaceful settlement; proposals and negotiation would serve to gain time to prepare for force and lay the foundation to justify its use. This position, of course, was radically different from that of the U.S. and the Labour Party.

3. THE FRENCH POSITION

For its own reasons, France's policy in the Suez Crisis closely paralleled Britain's. This similarity in view fostered close collabor-

[20] Great Britain, H.C. Deb., vol. 557, vol. 1609–17, 2 August, 1956, in *Documents on International Affairs*, p. 137.

[21] Eden, pp. 71, 356.

ation and eventual joint intervention. For France, too, Nasser was
the primary target.

Of course, the Canal takeover jeopardized substantial French
economic interests. Canal traffic was important for France, though
less so than for Britain: about 48 per cent of the French oil supply
came through the Canal. Moreover, some 80,000 French investors
held about half the shares of the Canal Company. Its main office
was in Paris, and its general manager was French.

Yet deep antagonism to Nasser was the prime factor in French
policy. The key to that hostility was the Algerian rebellion which
had erupted in late 1954. Despite heavily expanded forces, France
had failed to suppress the rebels. In their frustration, French
leaders, including Mollet, attributed their failure largely to
Nasser's support for the Algerian rebels. For some time, Egypt
had indeed provided supplies, succour, and encouragement to the
Algerian nationalists. In March 1956, Pineau, the Foreign Minister, had visited Cairo mainly to discuss Algeria. On his return to
Paris, he had told the National Assembly that Nasser had assured
him that Egypt was not training Algerian guerrillas, but Nasser
had made no similar pledge about shipping arms. Like Eden,
Mollet and his colleagues applied the Hitler analogy to Nasser,
whom they suspected of wide ambitions to dominate the Middle
East and north Africa.[22] They became firmly convinced that dis-
posing of Nasser was the way to defeat the Algerian rebellion.
Robert Lacoste, the French Resident Minister in Algeria, was later
quoted as saying: 'Better one French division in Egypt than four
divisions in Algeria.'[23]

Thus for France, the nationalizing of the Canal presented both
a provocation and a pretext. 'If Egypt were allowed to succeed in
grabbing the Canal [said Pineau], the Algerian nationalists would
take fresh heart.' Beyond that was the urge to wipe out the memory
of a succession of humiliating failures: the defeat of 1940; Indo-
China; Morocco and Tunisia. The French desperately needed a
victory to bolster their self-esteem. Interviews taken at the peak of
the Suez Crisis are highly revealing of the state of mind of the
French élite. 'We are trying to turn history back, to wipe out the
stains of Munich which led to our defeat in 1940 and of our
failure to prevent Hitler from taking over the Rhineland in 1936.

[22] Eisenhower, p. 36.
[23] Merry and Serge Bromberger, *Secrets of Suez* (Pan Books, London, 1957),
p. 52.

... Nasser is the symbol of all France's enemies ... of all France's humiliation in the past.'[24]

The French handling of the crisis was also influenced by its close ties with Israel, which enjoyed public sympathy deriving from the Nazi period and from left-wing interest in its socialist ideals. From 1954 on, the Franco-Israeli links grew closer, leading to substantial arms sales, including an agreement to furnish planes in November 1955.[25] These tendencies were strengthened in February 1956 when Guy Mollet, a socialist and a strong supporter of Israel, became Premier. Above all, France and Israel saw Nasser as the common enemy. That shared hostility was the decisive factor in the concerted military operation of October 1956. The French were less inhibited than the British were about co-operating directly with Israel to defeat Nasser. Britain did not want to alienate other Arab states; France had hardly any standing left to lose by intervening with Israel.

For all these reasons, the French reactions to the crisis were dictated primarily by political considerations, with legal factors playing little part in their decisions. In his first comment on the take-over of the Canal, on 28 July, Pineau stated that the French government refused to accept a unilateral act which was 'less legal than political' and tended to threaten freedom of passage through the Canal.[26] On 2 August, however, the French Assembly in expressing its 'indignation' asserted that 'Nasser had violated his obligations and the rules of international law in enforcing discrimination [against Israel] in Canal traffic; that he had proclaimed his intention to establish his hegemony in the Arab world; and that he constituted, by his conduct, a permanent threat to peace.' Confirming its 'determination not to yield to the *fait accompli*, [it asked] that the most energetic measures be taken to this end ...'[27]

The next day, Pineau's speech to the Assembly laid out clearly the government's approach to the crisis. The main theme was that Nasser could not be trusted to provide dependable guarantees for use of the Canal, recognized as necessary since the Convention of 1888. His 'word of honour' had been shown to be unreliable. In

[24] Herbert Luethy and David Rodnick, *French Motivation in the Suez Crisis* (The Institute for International Social Research, Princeton, N.J., 1956), p. 80.

[25] Pineau, Ben-Gurion, and Bar-Zohar interviews in Moncrieff, pp. 62–8.

[26] France, *Journal officiel* (Débats parlementaires), 29 July 1956, p. 3721, in *Documents on International affairs*, pp. 118–19.

[27] France, *Journal officiel* (Débats parlementaires), 2 August 1956, p. 3847, ibid., pp. 137–8.

March he had given 'his word of honour' that rebels were not being trained in Egypt; yet special surveillance in the following weeks had satisfied France that some Algerians were getting military training in Egyptian camps. Moreover, Nasser had blocked passage by Israeli ships despite the Convention of 1888 and the 1951 Security Council decision. And confidence in him had also been undermined by the way he had taken the Canal action and announced it to his people. It was one thing to nationalize a domestic utility. It was wholly different to nationalize an international utility protected by treaty. That was conceivable only after consulting with interested governments and fixing certain guarantees regarding its operation and the respect for the essential treaty provisions. Nasser had 'taken no account of these elementary rules of international law. He has not hesitated to give a political pretext for an act which he now pretends to be only a simple legal act.'[28]

Pineau's speech of 3 August set the stage for the later use of force. He referred to 'the acts of a fascist dictator', explicitly evoking the lessons of 1936 when failure to block Hitler had led inevitably to the Second World War. He cited the Anglo-French unanimity on the gravity of Nasser's action, while calling the U.S. less decisive. The Tripartite talks (see Chapter III) had, however, produced the joint Statement of 2 August as well as agreement on the plan for an international regime to safeguard Canal usage. The text showed 'clearly that [the takeover] violates the Convention of 1888'. That part, he said, might seem 'too legalistic to some', but it was essential to refute views that Nasser's action was legal. In essence, the choice was clear: either Nasser would back down and completely reverse his actions; or if he did not, 'every measure should be taken to force him to submit'. The French government could not, in any manner or form whatever, accept the Egyptian decision, and it would use all means necessary to defeat it.

Quite clearly, the French and British appraisals and conclusions reinforced each other. Both states saw Nasser as jeopardizing the entire Western position in the Middle East. To temporize would be to repeat the mistakes of the Hitler period. Nasser must be discredited, not appeased. Forcing him to accept international control of the Canal would humiliate him; if he refused to accept it, he must be compelled to back down, by force if necessary.

[28] France, *Journal officiel* (Débats parlementaires), 4 Aug. 1956, pp. 3868–73, ibid., pp. 140–50.

4. THE UNITED STATES POSITION

U.S. policy in the Suez Crisis was largely dominated by the effort to resolve the dispute by peaceful means and prevent resort to force. That objective reflected various considerations, but a major factor was Eisenhower's strong commitment to the U.N. Charter obligations against resort to force. The President took an active role in handling the crisis and in setting the policy line. As always, he worked closely with Dulles and depended heavily on him for managing the tactics and negotiations. Apparently, there were no significant differences in approach to the issues; yet the President was clearly in charge. Indeed, he was largely on his own for the first several days of the crisis when Dulles was absent in Latin America, and later in the critical U.N. phase after 3 November when Dulles was in hospital. Within the State Department, the person who worked most closely with Dulles in handling the crisis was Herman Phleger, the Legal Adviser of the Department.

The divergences between the United States and Britain and France emerged almost at once. They differed greatly in their appraisals of the issues, the objectives, and the appropriate means. For this, there were many reasons.

Unlike Britain and France, the United States had not been intimately involved with the Middle East over a long period. Even after the Second World War, the U.S. had at first tended to follow the British lead. And when action was required, the U.S. sought to act jointly with Britain and France, as in the Tripartite Declaration of 1950, adopted after the Arab–Israeli hostilities to preserve peace and restrain arms competition in the area. But, more and more, events forced the U.S. to define its own course.

Even so, U.S. concern with the Middle East was mainly derivative. Its direct interests were more limited than those of its allies. While U.S. shipping was a large Canal user and U.S. business had oil concessions, neither was crucial for the United States economy. Less directly, the U.S. had substantial interests of several kinds. Since its European allies depended so heavily on the Canal and the oil, their reliable access to both became an important interest for the U.S. And the security of Turkey, Iran, and the region as a whole was related to the U.S. containment policy, and was thought to require at least some Middle East participation, if only to provide greater depth of defence.

The United States had to pursue these interests in the context of its global strategy and especially of its struggle to contain the U.S.S.R. In particular, the U.S. was concerned that some actions in the Middle East might facilitate Soviet penetration there or have damaging repercussions outside the area. Efforts to balance the various U.S. objectives were complicated by the Arab–Israeli conflict and by Arab rivalries, as well as by the strong nationalist and anti-colonial attitudes found not only in the Middle East but throughout the newly independent areas of Asia and Africa. The U.S. seemed more sensitive to these attitudes than its allies, and more hopeful of appeasing them. In the Anglo-Egyptian base negotiations, the U.S. had encouraged Britain to agree to the Egyptian demand for full withdrawal from the Suez base. And to the annoyance of the British, it had refrained from joining the Baghdad defence pact, which Nasser attacked as 'imperialism' or 'neo-colonialism'.

Nevertheless, relations with Nasser steadily deteriorated. During 1955, his harshest blow to U.S. policy was the Soviet arms deal: at one stroke that brought the U.S.S.R into the Middle East, linked the major Arab state to the Soviet bloc, and upset the arms balance between Israel and the Arabs. Even so, the U.S. continued to compete for Egyptian allegiance by not selling matching arms to Israel, and by the joint offer (with the U.K. and I.B.R.D.) to help Egypt finance the Aswan Dam. By spring 1956, however, readiness to placate Nasser had been chilled by his insistent anti-Western actions. In withdrawing the Aswan offer in mid-July, the U.S. stressed that Egypt's arms commitments had mortgaged its national income so heavily as to leave inadequate resources for the dam project. Besides, the U.S. Congress was hostile towards aid to Egypt, and Dulles was also concerned lest allies should conclude that blackmail paid better than co-operation. Thus, the U.S. had lost hope of good relations with Nasser even before he nationalized the Canal Company.

The British and French reaction to Nasser's move forced the U.S. to decide quickly on its objectives in handling the crisis and on suitable means for achieving them.

The first reports left little doubt that the British and French were determined to depose or discredit Nasser and to resort to force for that purpose, if necessary. In his cable of 27 July, already mentioned, Eden had urged the need to 'take issue with Nasser on the broader international grounds'; not to 'allow ourselves to be-

come involved in legal quibbles about the right ... to nationalize';
and to 'be ready, in the last resort, to use force to bring Nasser to
his senses', as the British were 'prepared to do' and were making 'a
military plan accordingly'.[29]

Even more explicit were the cables from Robert Murphy, whom
the President had sent at once to London. As Murphy recalled,
'I was left in no doubt [by Macmillan] that the British Government
believed that Suez was a test which could be met only by the use of
force.' Macmillan later quoted and confirmed this impression, adding 'I made it quite clear that we and France must accept the challenge, or sink into the rank of second-class nations.' Indeed,
Eisenhower's letter of 31 July to Eden was prompted by 'the
messages, communicated to me through Murphy from you and
Harold Macmillan, telling me on a most secret basis of your decision to employ force without delay or attempting any intermediate
or less drastic steps'. Macmillan's own conviction was that 'neither
[Dulles] nor Eisenhower could ever have been under any misapprehension. Britain and France in the long run would not shrink
from force.' The French government, Eisenhower wrote later, 'took
an even more emotional view than the British', comparing Nasser's
action to the 'seizure of the Rhineland by Hitler two decades
earlier'.[30]

Eisenhower and Dulles took issue with the British and French
on both their analysis and their aims. Their position, as Eisenhower understood it, was (1) that Nasser 'had unilaterally flouted
a solemn treaty'; (2) that Egypt could not operate the Canal
efficiently and would not comply with the 1888 Convention; (3)
that success would so enhance Nasser's influence as essentially to
make him 'an Arab dictator controlling the Mediterranean' (which
Eisenhower 'suspected was the overriding' factor).

While recognizing the disastrous consequences of 'any closing
of the Canal', Eisenhower believed that this analysis was over-
drawn. According to him, the United States differed profoundly
with its allies on each count. (1) It 'doubted the validity of [their]
legal position' on the seizure and on resort to force. Although the
Canal was 'a utility essential to global welfare', the 'inherent
right' of Egypt to nationalize it 'could scarcely be doubted'. (2) The
main issue, therefore, was whether or not Nasser would operate

---

[29] Eden, p. 477.

[30] Robert Murphy, *Diplomat Among Warriors* (Doubleday, Garden City,
N.Y., 1964), p. 380; Macmillan, pp. 103–4; Eisenhower. pp. 664–5, 36.

it in conformity with the Convention of 1888. That could only be determined by experience. On the basis of his Panama service, Eisenhower questioned the view that Egypt could not operate the Canal efficiently. (3) The U.K. and France were grossly exaggerating the broader threat of Nasser, especially in comparing him to Hitler. Any resort to force, as the case then stood, would not be warranted or sensible. It would weaken, and perhaps even destroy, the United Nations. Force should be considered, if at all, only after every resource for a peaceful settlement had been exhausted.[31]

Starting on 31 July, by letter and through Dulles and the press, Eisenhower sought to persuade the British and French on two key points: to restrict their objective to ensuring the reliable functioning of the Canal, without trying to depose Nasser; and to refrain from resort to force. As he put it to Eden:

We have two problems, the first of which is the assurance of permanent and efficient operation on the Suez Canal with justice for all concerned. The second is to see that Nasser shall not grow as a menace to the peace and vital interests of the West. In my view, these two problems need not and possibly cannot be solved simultaneously and by the same methods, although we are exploring further means to this end. The first is the most important for the moment and must be solved in such a way as not to make the second more difficult. Above all, there must be no grounds for our several peoples to believe that anyone is using the Canal difficulty as an excuse to proceed forcibly against Nasser. And we have friends in the Middle East who tell us they would like to see Nasser's deflation brought about. But they seem unanimous in feeling that the Suez is not the issue on which to attempt to do this by force.[32]

His reasons for opposing force included the following: failure to exhaust peaceful means in conformity with the U.N. Charter would outrage public opinion in the United States and elsewhere; use of force would revive memories of imperialism and colonialism, offending many newer nations, and would drive the Arabs, including those hostile to Nasser, to unite behind him; it would risk closing the Canal and becoming bogged down in guerrilla warfare; it would facilitate Soviet penetration of the Middle East as a supporter of Arab independence; and it would create a precedent for resorting to force to solve other problems, as in Korea, Taiwan,

---

[31] Eisenhower, p. 39.
[32] Eisenhower, letter to Eden, 2 Sept. 1956, in Eisenhower, pp. 666–8 (quotation on 667).

and elsewhere.[32a] Accordingly, any use of force was conceivable only under '*extreme* circumstances', which would not arise if Egypt could operate the Canal, and if it complied with the 1888 Convention.[33]

Capitulation to Nasser would also be unsound, in the President's view. A unified front by those dependent on the Canal should succeed in inducing a satisfactory solution peacefully. There were many means of pressure, including user co-operation, economic measures, exploitation of Arab rivalries, and development of newer tankers and pipelines. 'Even though this procedure may fail to give the set-back to Nasser that he so much deserves, we can better retrieve our position subsequently than if military force were hastily invoked.'[34] Since this approach clashed with that of Britain and France, the U.S. task was both complex and delicate: to frustrate resort to force by Britain and France without a split, and to resolve the Canal issue peacefully.

In defining its legal position, the U.S. also had to follow a narrow path. The starting point was the U.N. obligation to settle disputes by peaceful means 'in conformity with the principles of justice and international law' and to refrain from 'the threat or use of force' contrary to the U.N. Purposes. In the initial phase, however, the U.S. did not want to involve the U.N. in the crisis. In his press conference of 8 August, President Eisenhower said that it would be better in the early stages of the crisis to get the interested parties together to work out a settlement (in keeping with Article 33 of the Charter), especially since action in the United Nations would be impeded by the Security Council veto.[35] The U.S. did not want to see the U.N. dragged into the crisis prematurely and be unable to resolve it. Dulles considered the United Nations as an arbiter of last resort, to be used only if the interested parties proved incapable of resolving the problem. He did, however, envision the U.N. as fulfilling a supervisory role in the eventual settlement.

The main difficulty was to devise a 'theory of the case' against Nasser. Eisenhower and Dulles fully understood the distrust of Nasser by the U.K., France, and other users, and their desire to assure efficient and fair operation of the Canal by safeguards more

---

[32a] These reasons are analysed more fully in Chapter IV, Section 2.
[33] Eisenhower, p. 44.
[34] Eisenhower, letter to Eden, 2 Sept. 1956, ibid., p. 667.
[35] Department of State, *Suez*, p. 46.

solid than Nasser's promise to comply with the 1888 Convention. Yet it was hard to fault the nationalization as such, especially since fair compensation seemed to be tendered. Moreover, any demand to restore the Canal to the Company would have been unwise politically, and in any case, would only have put off the problem until the Concession expired in 1968.

Another obvious approach was to claim that user dependence on the Canal made it an international public utility which the world community was entitled to regulate. The United States was deterred from adopting this theory by its interests in the Panama Canal. For the U.S. that Canal had a strategic importance rather different from the Suez Canal's importance for Egypt. Since the U.S. was not prepared to accept international operation or control of Panama, it could not rely on a general claim of global interest in Suez. Hence the U.S. had to base the Suez case on the treaties specific to Suez, taking the tenuous line that the treaty status of Panama was wholly different.

In consequence, Dulles sought to show that the Convention of 1888 (as its preamble said) had 'completed the system' for the Suez Canal regime, which rested partly on the Concession and operation by the Canal Company. But this argument had an obvious and substantial weakness. The Convention doubtless assumed the existence of the Concession until 1968; yet it expressly provided that the expiration of the Concession should not affect the continuance of the Convention. Thus it was not wholly convincing to argue that the early ending of the Concession violated the Convention. In practical terms, however, there was a difference. As 1968 approached, users would either have been able to negotiate some further safeguards for reliable operation of the Canal, or would have had time to adjust their patterns of shipping and trade. The abruptness of the takeover denied the users these alternatives and undermined confidence. But if abrupt termination was a violation of the Convention, that was a rather flimsy ground to justify international operation.

III

EFFORTS FOR PEACEFUL SOLUTION

FOR three months after the Canal takeover, Dulles tried to devise formulas which would mobilize pressure on Nasser to negotiate, guarantee secure use of the Canal, and forestall British–French military action. But this alchemy could not combine the diverse elements of the situation into a stable compound. Eventually, the mixture exploded.

The U.S. premiss was that negotiations and time would reduce the danger of bellicose action and make possible some kind of non-violent settlement with Egypt.[1] Tactically, Eisenhower and Dulles sought to induce and extend negotiations and peaceful processes, hoping thereby to make it harder to resort to force. At the same time, they sought to build up the pressure on Nasser to negotiate, through public opinion, economic coercion, and fear or uncertainty about the threat of force.

These twin aims were hard to combine. If the sense of crisis and tension were relaxed, Nasser would incline towards intransigence. And if it were heightened, Britain and France would exploit it to justify force. Dulles would doubtless have preferred to have the threat of force in the background as leverage on Nasser, but he feared that Eden would claim the United States had acquiesced in the ultimate resort to force if the U.S. position were left ambiguous. Prodded by the French, Eden was seeking to bring the dispute to a head by showing that a peaceful solution was hopeless, while Dulles was trying throughout to prevent that result while at the same time attempting to induce Nasser to make concessions which would offer adequate safeguards for the future operation of the Canal.

Inevitably, this basic divergence of purpose produced frustration and distrust for both the United States and its allies. The period from the Canal seizure to the Israeli attack in October became a sort of duel between Eden and Dulles. Dulles used all his ingenuity to devise proposals and methods to gain time and the chance for

[1] Robert Murphy, *Diplomat Among Warriors*, p. 384.

a peaceful solution. For Eden, any settlement would be a defeat if it did not discredit Nasser; therefore he sought to shape and utilize each proposal so as to achieve that result or justify military action by its failure.

1. PROPOSAL FOR AN INTERNATIONAL AGENCY

Tripartite talks. Dulles's efforts began on 31 July when he went to London for three days of talks with the British and French. They forcefully repeated the views and intentions already conveyed by letter and through Murphy: their entire position in the Middle East would be destroyed if Nasser were allowed 'to get away with it', and they would do whatever was necessary to prevent that result. Dulles sought to reassure them that the United States shared their concern about the takeover of the Canal while strongly discouraging their use of force. He agreed that it was intolerable for the Suez Canal to be dominated by one nation without international controls and that Nasser should be compelled 'to disgorge'. But it was essential to exhaust every avenue for a peaceful solution before even considering force.

The outcome of the Tripartite talks marked an apparent success for Dulles's policy of restraint and negotiation. By their close on 3 August, the Three Powers had agreed to call a conference of twenty-four concerned maritime powers (including Egypt)[1a] for later in August, to consider what 'steps should be taken to establish operating arrangements under an international system designed to assure the continuity of operation of the Canal as guaranteed by the Convention of 1888, consistently with legitimate Egyptian interests'.[2] The Three also agreed to submit to the conference a proposal for an international agency to operate the Canal.

The proposal to transfer the Canal to an international agency epitomized the dilemma inherent in the U.S. approach. For the users, this was doubtless the surest way to protect against Egypt's misuse of the Canal to exercise leverage on users. But for Nasser, such a solution would amount to virtual capitulation, which

[1a] Eight were chosen as signers (or successors) of the Convention of 1888; eight on the basis of shipping using the Canal; and eight on the basis of trade dependence on it. Invited were Australia, Ceylon, Denmark, Egypt, Ethiopia, the Federal Republic of Germany, France, Greece, India, Indonesia, Iran, Italy, Japan, the Netherlands, New Zealand, Norway, Pakistan, Portugal, the Soviet Union, Spain, Sweden, Turkey, the United Kingdom, and the United States. Egypt and Greece refused to attend.

[2] The quotation is from Department of State, *Suez*, p. 35.

would discredit him and undermine his prestige. That, of course, was why this solution was acceptable to the British and French: Nasser could agree to it only as the last alternative to his overthrow.

Eisenhower was concerned by this dilemma. During the London Conference, when Dulles cabled him the text of the Tripartite proposal, he questioned whether Nasser could accept an *operating* agency, and suggested instead a 'supervisory' board, with a manager appointed by Nasser, subject to board approval. When Dulles replied that Britain would probably reject such a solution, Eisenhower authorized him to accept the original text if necessary.

Dulles may have been pursuing a more complex tactic. His first problem was to focus on the Canal dispute, to start negotiations, and to unify the main users. He may have thought of the proposal for an 'international agency' as only an opening gambit designed to meet these needs. Once under way, a negotiation might work out some compromise form of operation of the Canal 'under an international system' which would adequately safeguard the users, without explicitly reversing the nationalization. Thus for Dulles the 'international operation' would be a *maximum* position, from which he could retreat to 'supervision' or other forms of participation in Egyptian operation of the Canal. Indeed, later in the controversy Dulles made clear his receptivity to variations of an 'international system' short of operation by an international agency. But his maximum position was the *minimum* position for the U.K. and France. Any compromise which would not be a major defeat for Nasser would, therefore, be intolerable for them.

The hope of getting a negotiation started also depended on Nasser. To encourage his compliance, American policy hung back in applying economic and political pressures on Egypt. After the trilateral talks, the U.S. even removed the restrictions on trade with Egypt which had been 'temporarily' instituted on 1 August and freed the assets of the Suez Canal Company.

After the talks, Dulles sought to create a propitious setting for the conference. He expressed optimism about its ability to work out a solution acceptable to all parties concerned. In a television report on his return to the U.S. on 3 August, Dulles described the crisis as 'dangerous'. All possible solutions appeared to have grave disadvantages, and he did not want to commit himself prematurely. He did, however, stress two major points. First, he expected Egypt to take seriously the conference's proposal if for no other reason than the weight of world opinion which it would carry. Secondly, the U.S. had made no commitments on possible actions should the conference fail. The first statement was clearly designed to bring pressure to bear on Egypt, while the second warned the U.K. and France that the United States would not be committed to the use of force, in the event that the conference failed.

Dulles also set about mobilizing diplomatic support wherever possible for an acceptable non-violent settlement at the London Conference. He conferred with twenty Latin American ambassadors, while his associates talked with those of Saudi Arabia, Japan, Lebanon, India, Tunisia, and Australia. Israel was discouraged from raising the issue of the Egyptian blockade of Israeli shipping, lest it prejudice some states against an international agency. American negotiations with Saudi Arabia over a possible air-base at Dhahran were suspended during this period of the crisis. Hints appeared in the press about future U.N. economic sanctions, or possible British–French recourse to arms under Article 51 of the United Nations Charter, if the conference failed.[3]

The London Conference, 16–23 August. The purpose of the conference was to unite the main user nations on a common approach.

The prospects for the conference were uncertain. As early as 4 August, Nasser had publicly threatened to fight if the West persisted in its demand for international control of the Canal. Worse still, Eden's speech on 8 August condemning Nasser presaged the possible use of force unless the conference agreed on international control. On 12 August, Nasser had refused to attend the conference and described the proposal as 'collective colonialism'.[4] Meanwhile, Britain and France pressed their military preparations, having already dispatched air and naval forces towards the Middle East. Despite these omens, the conference was a substantial success. In the end, eighteen of the twenty-two participants (all except Ceylon, India, Indonesia, and the U.S.S.R.) agreed to a slightly amended Tripartite proposal for international control and operation.

Dulles took a leading role in the conference. On the first day, he presented the Tripartite proposal which stated certain prin-

---

[3] *N.Y. Times*, 5, 7, and 8 Aug. 1956.
[4] Herman Finer, *Dulles Over Suez: The Theory and Practice of His Diplomacy* (Quadrangle Books, Chicago, 1964), pp. 114–31; *N.Y. Times*, 9 Aug. 1956; Department of State, *Suez*, pp. 47–52.

ciples to govern the Canal 'system', and called for entrusting its operation to an international board, to be established by treaty and associated with the United Nations. The principles he stated for a settlement were as follows:

First, the Canal should be operated efficiently as a free, secure, international waterway in accordance with the principles of the Suez Convention of 1888. Second, the operation should be divorced from the influence of national politics, from whatever source derived. Third, there should be recognition and satisfaction of all legitimate rights and interests of Egypt in the Canal and in its operation, including an equitable and fair return. Fourth, provision should be made for the payment of fair compensation to the Universal Suez Company.[5]

Dulles stressed the imperative necessity of creating a 'definite system, designed to guarantee at all times and for all Powers the free use of the Suez Maritime Canal'. Other nations, he declared, could not be asked to assume the role of petitioners to Egypt's whim for their use of the Canal. Dulles considered as the absolute minimum 'a permanent operation of the Canal under an international system which will, in fact, give confidence to those who would normally wish to use the Canal'.[6] Under the Tripartite proposal, these results would be achieved by creating (1) a Suez Canal Board, composed of the users and Egypt, with authority to manage and develop the Canal; (2) an Arbitral Commission to settle disputes; and (3) effective sanctions for any violation of the Convention.

The Soviet Union and India criticized the proposal as unacceptable to Egypt; and India submitted an alternative based on amending the 1888 Convention and forming a consultative group of users. In rejecting these criticisms, Dulles said, 'I suggest ... that any expression of our views ought not to be based on speculation as to what the Government of Egypt will or will not agree to.'[7]

Although unacceptable to Russia and India, an international authority did appeal to most other nations present. Hence Dulles pressed forward with this plan to keep together as large a group of them as possible, hoping that a clear consensus would induce Nasser to open negotiations with the collective body of users. Dulles was especially anxious to rally support from the new and

[5] Document SUEZ/56/V/2 and amendments, in Department of State, *Suez*, pp. 77–8.
[6] Ibid., pp. 75, 76.
[7] Document SUEZ/56/V/5, in Department of State, *Suez*, p. 179.

less developed nations, which supported Nasser's right to nationalize, so as to counter charges of neo-colonialism or domination.
Thus, in arguing for the proposed international agency, he stressed
that reliable passage was the crucial issue, and that Egypt would
continue to own the Canal under international operation. The
draft proposal was largely limited to basic principles which could
be developed in direct negotiations with Nasser. Dulles accepted
minor amendments to his draft suggested by Ethiopia, Iran, Pakistan, and Turkey to preserve consensus among the large majority
of the Canal users. And at the close of the conference on 23 August,
despite opposition by India and the U.S.S.R., eighteen of the
twenty-two nations, representing over 90 per cent of the Canal
traffic, approved what became known as the Eighteen-Power Proposal. Spain offered an alternative, calling for user members on
the Egyptian Board, which it asked to be submitted if the Eighteen-
Power Proposal were rejected.[8]

   The Menzies mission. The Eighteen appointed a committee of
five (Australia, Ethiopia, Iran, Sweden, and the United States),
headed by Sir Robert Menzies, the Prime Minister of Australia,
to present the proposal to Nasser. Their mandate was specific and
limited. They were to submit the proposal to Egypt, explain its
purposes and objectives, and find out if Egypt would negotiate a
convention 'on the basis thereof'. If so, further arrangements would
be made with Egypt for going ahead. In other words, the Committee was not authorized to negotiate or to deviate from the formal
proposal or to discuss any changes in its terms. For the British and
French, this restricted mandate was critically important, for it
removed the risk of watering down the plan for turning the Canal
over to an international agency.[9] Yet it could have impeded getting
a negotiation started if Nasser had been interested in doing so.

   Eden and Macmillan urged Dulles to head the mission, but he
refused, probably to avoid engaging his own prestige in its success
(which was highly doubtful), thereby making it harder for him to
push alternative means to avoid force if this proposal was rejected.
Dulles presented the prospects of the Menzies mission hopefully,
however; on his return to Washington on 25 August, he said: 'We
hope that the Government of Egypt will respect the opinions thus
soberly but firmly expressed and responsibly make its own indis-

   [8] Conference Document, SUEZ/56/D/25, ibid., p. 293; Conference Document, SUEZ/56/D/13, ibid., pp. 292-3.
   [9] Conference Document, SUEZ/56/D/25, ibid., p. 293; Eden, p. 506.

pensable contribution to the peaceful solution which is enjoined by the principles and purposes of the United Nations.'[10]

Dulles was still struggling to overcome the dilemma of U.S. policy: to obtain concessions from Nasser while opposing force. In this effort he sought to reduce the crisis to manageable proportions by a twofold approach. First, he attempted to focus on specific issues so as to defuse the situation. Shortly after returning from the London Conference, Dulles told reporters:

I don't think it's necessary to think of the problem in terms of these very great issues, these great slogans of 'nationalism versus internationalism', or 'nationalism versus colonialism,' or 'Asia versus Europe,' or any such things. Then the problem becomes almost insoluble. But when you begin to think of the concrete practical things you have to do to establish confidence that there will be an impartial, competent, and efficient operation of the Canal, then I think the matter should be soluble.[11]

Second, Dulles tried to de-escalate the crisis further by taking it out of the Cold War context of East–West rivalry. He sought to do this by downgrading both the United States and Russia as principal parties to the dispute. In a post-Conference news briefing on 28 August, Dulles played down U.S. interest by asserting that 'the question of what arrangements about operations would be satisfactory is not primarily a question for the United States to answer', since the U.S. was not greatly dependent upon the use of the Canal. He then sought to drive a wedge between the U.S.S.R. and Egypt by implying that Soviet propaganda, carried on against the Eighteen-Power Proposal even during the London Conference, made it harder for Egypt to accept a 'fair plan'. In Dulles's assessment, the major factors which impeded a 'just' settlement of the Suez Crisis were political concerns having to do with national prestige, leadership roles, and Cold War rivalries.[12]

The Menzies mission fared poorly in Egypt. By 7 September, talks had made it crystal clear that Nasser would not accept the Eighteen-Power Proposal as a basis for negotiation. Nor did he pick up the Spanish proposal for putting user members on the Egyptian Board. Menzies sent him letters summarizing the content of the discussions and the arguments for the specific proposals. In them, he identified two features as the crux of the proposal: (1) the principle of insulating the Canal from politics; and (2) operation

---

[10] Department of State Press Release No. 450, 28 Aug. 1956, in *Suez*, p. 295.
[11] Ibid., p. 296. [12] Ibid., pp. 295–301.

by an international agency as the means for doing so. Both, he wrote, were essential to inspire the 'world-wide confidence' necessary to reassure the users and to find financing for the expansion of the Canal.[13]

Nasser's reply of 9 September restated his reasons for rejecting the proposal while accepting most of the guiding principles of the eighteen. Basically, he asserted that operation by an international board would take the Canal away from Egypt and put it under the control of a group of users. Such 'collective domination' would be 'self-defeating'. It would infringe on Egyptian sovereignty and would not insulate the Canal from politics but rather create 'incalculable strife' and 'plunge the Suez Canal into the turmoil of politics'. The Egyptian people, whose willing co-operation was essential for Canal operation, would consider such a system hostile and offensive to their rights and dignity. Once more Nasser blamed the British and French for manufacturing the crisis by threats and military preparations, economic sanctions, and so forth, despite the continued orderly functioning of the Canal without discrimination. Finally, Nasser stated that Egypt, which was deeply interested in the efficient and progressive management of the Canal, was ready to revise and reaffirm the Convention of 1888 to assure freedom of passage, to make binding arrangements regarding fair tolls, and to carry out the development programme of the former Canal Company and earmark an adequate share of revenues therefor.[14]

On 10 September, Egypt sent many states a proposal for a new Suez conference to resolve the issues of freedom of passage, future development, and equitable tolls, 'without prejudice to Egypt's sovereignty or dignity'.[15] This proposal was not taken up.

2. SUEZ CANAL USERS' ASSOCIATION

The failure of the Menzies mission inevitably posed the question: what next? Even before the mission left for Cairo, the British and French had begun to consider that question. The effort to find an answer produced new frictions and frustrations between the U.S. and the British and French. For one thing, despite strenuous urging by the latter powers, the United States refused to order its ships to cease paying Canal tolls to Nasser.

[13] Suez Committee Document SC/D/ 29, ibid., p. 312.
[14] Suez Committee Document SC/D/33, ibid., pp. 317–22.
[15] Ibid., pp. 327–30.

More crucial were differences about an appeal to the U.N. Security Council. Considering this step as a futile but necessary prelude to resort to force, the British wanted to take it promptly 'before the possibility of military action slipped from our grasp'. Delay would make it harder. 'In a few weeks [after the end of August] we should be poised to strike, if we had to strike. It would be costly to keep up this position indefinitely.' On 28 August, the British decided to go to the Security Council as soon as the Menzies mission was completed, and they requested the U.S. to agree. Dulles raised various objections to the draft resolution and the timing; but he agreed to support it 'on the understanding that our move was an honest attempt to reach a solution and not a "device of obtaining cover" '. A few days later, however, the appeal was put off because the U.S. refused to bind itself in advance not to accept in the U.N. (1) any solution short of the Eighteen-Power Proposal, and (2) any limitation on freedom of action.[16]

The divergence of views was further underscored by an exchange of letters between Eisenhower and Eden at this time. On 2 September, the President told Eden 'that American public opinion flatly rejects the thought of using force' and advised separating the Canal dispute from the long-term problems of Nasser's aims. In his reply, Eden explicitly invoked the analogy to Hitler as showing that the specific dispute must not be treated in isolation since it was 'the opening gambit in a planned campaign designed by Nasser to expel all Western influence and interests from Arab countries. There are risks in using force to defeat Nasser, but they will be less now than after delay.'[17]

To fill the policy vacuum, Dulles on 4 September suggested the formation of a Suez Canal Users' Association (S.C.U.A.), a concept he had devised during a brief stay at his Canadian island retreat. His theory was that since the 1888 Convention entitled the users to transit the Canal, they could band together to form a co-operative to exercise their rights under the Convention. Then they could hire pilots, organize convoys, collect dues, and pay Egypt its compensation, and generally represent the group in dealing with the Egyptian authority. The scheme was recognized as provisional, but it might hold together the users for negotiation or for any proceedings in the U.N., and it might lead to alternatives for a solution.[18]

[16] Quotations are from Eden, pp. 530, 509, 513.
[17] Eisenhower, p. 667; Eden, p. 521.   [18] Eisenhower, pp. 672–5.

The S.C.U.A. scheme proved an apple of discord between the U.S. and its allies, largely as a result of their divergent purposes. The details of Dulles's plan for S.C.U.A. reached Eden and Selwyn Lloyd on 10 September, while they were consulting with Mollet and Pineau. For the French, the proposal had little appeal; it was premissed upon Egyptian co-operation, but why should that be expected now if it had not been forthcoming when Menzies presented the Eighteen-Power Proposal? If the U.S. would not countenance force, as the President insisted, and Nasser would not accept S.C.U.A. freely, what progress did the Users' Association represent? The British, it seemed to their French allies, were being naïve or sentimental in hoping to entangle the United States with Anglo-French policy through the Users' Association. If British domestic politics required an appeal to the Security Council, this should be made forthwith, despite American qualms. When the Security Council reached its inevitable deadlock, the military action (known as Musketeer) would remain as the only alternative.

Eden accepted the S.C.U.A. idea, however, apparently hoping thereby to create conditions for the use of force should Nasser refuse to accept the plan. In presenting the S.C.U.A. proposal to the House of Commons on 12 September, Eden emphasized the forceful interpretation which Britain and France wished to see in S.C.U.A. Amid cries of 'deliberate provocation!' and 'you are talking about war!' Eden said that if the Egyptian government should attempt to interfere with the Users' Association, then 'Her Majesty's Government and others concerned will be free to take such further steps ... as seem to be required ... either through the United Nations, or by other means, for the assertion of their rights.'[19]

The next day, at his press conference, Dulles's tone was quite different. He endorsed the Users' Association to act as agent for the users and to seek the co-operation of Egypt under the 1888 Convention. He stressed its practical, provisional character and denied any intent to impose a regime on Egypt. To Eden's dismay, he stated that if Egypt prevented passage, the U.S. would divert ships around the Cape. 'We do not intend to shoot our way through', even if blocked by force. That same day in the House of Commons the Leader of the Opposition rose to ask: 'Is he [the Prime Minister] prepared to say on behalf of Her Majesty's Government that

[19] Great Britain, H.C. Deb., vol. 558, col. 10–15, in *Documents on International Affairs*, p. 206.

they will not shoot their way through the Canal?' Eden would not give this assurance. Instead he asserted that complete understanding obtained between London and Washington; both agreed that if Nasser did not accept S.C.U.A. he would be in default of the 1888 Convention and the case would be taken to the Security Council.[20]

There were added frustrations, especially for Eden and Mollet. On 15 September, when the Western pilots left their Canal posts as directed by the Company, the effect was negligible. The Egyptians kept the traffic moving without serious delays or disruptions, with pilots recruited at home and abroad. Also on 15 September, Nasser denounced the S.C.U.A. proposal in a speech once again evoking the themes of imperialism, domination, independence, sovereignty, and Arab nationalism. And in statements and letters to the Prime Minister, the Soviet Union repeated the claim (first heard in the House of Commons) that S.C.U.A. was 'a dangerous provocation', and warned against any attack on Egypt. These various frustrations tended to reinforce the British and French resolve to pursue their policy to the end.

The Second London Conference, meeting from 19 to 22 September, was only a nominal success. While agreeing to create S.C.U.A., it could not bridge the deeper divergences which became steadily more manifest. For Eden, S.C.U.A. promised a means for withholding from Nasser any profit from the nationalization until a settlement had been reached that was acceptable to the West. And if Nasser should be provoked to deny passage, that could be treated as a violation of the Convention of 1888 and a ground for military action.

But Dulles took another tack, in part at least to achieve a consensus in the conference. He insisted that the payment of dues to S.C.U.A. had to be *voluntary* and declined to bring pressure to bear on American shippers. He would only initial the document which emerged from the conference if the voluntary nature of the association was expressed with the greatest clarity. It now seemed to the British that S.C.U.A. would be little more than 'an agency for collecting dues for Nasser'. Dulles, on the other hand, sought to stress the practical value of S.C.U.A. as a means for working with Egypt on the operating level. While reaffirming the earlier proposal for the international agency, he may well have

[20] Department of State Press Release No. 486, 13 Sept. 1956, in *Suez*, pp. 335–45; Eden, p. 538.

hoped that S.C.U.A. might lead to negotiations for more pragmatic piecemeal safeguards. As he said on 19 September:

This readiness of ours to cooperate with Egypt on a de facto provisional basis may also suggest a provisional solution which the United Nations might find it useful to invoke while the search for a permanent solution goes on. It has, I know, been the thinking of many of us that if the principal parties to the Suez dispute are unable to find a solution by means of their own choosing, that the offices of the United Nations should be availed of.[21]

And by keeping the eighteen users united, S.C.U.A. might improve the prospects for settlement in the U.N. Meanwhile, the joint study of substitutes for the Canal might also put some pressure on Nasser to reach a solution which would restore confidence.

Yet a solution seemed more elusive than ever. Nasser continued intransigent and defiant, and even more cocky as the Egyptians operated the Canal efficiently after the withdrawal of many foreign pilots. Time was working to reduce the sense of crisis and the pressure of world opinion on which Dulles counted. Sensing this, the British and French, with their military forces mobilized, would be tempted to strike without more delay.

Frustrated, Dulles pleaded with the conference to recognize that justice had to be accorded to both sides in order to achieve a non-violent settlement. American policy had fought hard, and would continue to fight, for a world in which disputes could be solved peaceably. But other nations had to complement America's policy of restraining Britain and France by bringing pressure to bear on Egypt. 'If you have a world in which force is not used, you must also have a world in which a just solution of problems of this sort can be achieved.' Invoking the United Nations Charter, Dulles argued that 'the very first article ... says that the purpose of the United Nations is to bring about settlements by "peaceful means, and in conformity with the principles of justice and international law". And if that latter part of it is forgotten, the first part of it will inevitably come to be ignored.'[22]

The formation of S.C.U.A., fixed for 1 October, failed to help in resolving the basic problem. In the eyes of Britain and France, the United States had watered down the initial purpose of S.C.U.A.

[21] Department of State Press Release No. 497, 20 Sept. 1956, in *Suez*, pp. 353-6.
[22] Department of State Press Release No. 498, 21 Sept. 1956, ibid., p. 362.

by disavowing any intent to coerce Nasser through withholding tolls or the threat of boycott. Thus the S.C.U.A. episode embittered the British especially and made them more ready to follow the French lead towards independent action.

As a counterweight, Dulles sought to soften Nasser by stressing the limits on peaceful efforts. At a news conference immediately after his return from the Conference, Dulles commented on the threat of war if Egypt continued to reject a solution based on justice and international law. Later, on 'Meet the Press', he confronted the issues even more forcefully when he stated: 'I don't think you can expect to go on forever asking people not to resort to force.'[23] His obvious hope was to bring pressure on Egypt to alter its intransigence while at the same time manoeuvring into a position once again to exercise leverage on his allies.

3. BRITISH–FRENCH APPEAL TO THE U.N.

On 12 September, Britain and France—considering a U.N. appeal as necessary before resorting to force, if only to show its futility—had brought the Suez dispute to the attention of the Security Council. In a joint letter to the President of the Council, they suggested that the refusal of the Egyptian government to negotiate on the basis of the Eighteen-Power Proposal constituted 'an aggravation of the situation which, if allowed to continue, would constitute a manifest danger to peace and security'.[24] On 23 September, they requested U.N. action without consultation with Dulles, who had just left London.

Their draft resolution, after reciting their view of the preceding background, (1) asserted the necessity for safeguards for the user's rights under the Convention of 1888; (2) endorsed the Eighteen-Power Proposal as a suitable solution; (3) urged Egypt to negotiate a system for the Canal on that basis; and (4) urged Egypt to co-operate with S.C.U.A. pending permanent settlement. Egypt at once filed a counter-protest against British and French military preparations and threats. Both items were scheduled for debate on 5 October.[25]

The public debate in the Security Council followed predictable

[23] *N.Y. Times*, 24 Sept. 1956.
[24] U.N. SCOR, 11th Year, Supplement for July, Aug., and Sept. 1956, Doc. S/3645, 12 Sept. 1956, in *Documents on International Affairs*, pp. 204–5.
[25] U.N. SCOR, 11th Year, 734th Meeting, 26 Sept. 1956, pp. 1–22.

lines. Britain and France restated their claim that Nasser's seizure
of the Canal was illegal in disrupting the 'international system'
established under the Convention of 1888. At stake was respect for
the rule of law and international obligations. For Egypt, the action
was a legitimate exercise of sovereignty over a domestic company
and did not affect the 1888 Convention, which Egypt continued
to respect and comply with. The proposal for international operation was a challenge to Egypt's sovereignty. The U.S.S.R. supported Egypt completely and attacked the resolution. Conversely,
the U.S. endorsed the resolution, elaborating Dulles's 'peace with
justice' theme as two sides of a coin. Probably Dulles's most significant comment, however, was that the Eighteen-Power Proposal
was *not* 'sacrosanct' or the sole means for carrying out the basic
principles. There were 'a great variety of means'; the Council
should consider 'any alternative suggestions'. This opened the
door to solutions based on Egyptian operation with institutional
safeguards to protect user interests.

Speaking for Egypt, Fawzi was also more flexible than hereto-
fore. According to Nutting, Nasser was under wide and growing
pressures to negotiate. The British financial measures were starting
to pinch, and the British–French denial of Canal dues was affecting two-thirds of the traffic. Moreover, Nasser was being pressed to
settle by some of the Arab oil states, and by the Soviet Union
(which faced unrest in Poland and Hungary), as well as by the
Indians and Tito. Finally, the French–British military threat had
not subsided with the passage of time. Whatever the reason, Fawzi
concluded his statement to the Council with a positive suggestion:

It is probably advisable, if we agree—as we seem to do—on negotiating
a peaceful settlement of this question, to establish a negotiating body of
reasonable size and, more important still, to put for the guidance of
that body a set of principles to work by and objectives to keep in mind
and attain. Fortunately there are basic principles and objectives on
which no disagreement at all exists, and which will secure our unanimous approval.

The key principles were (1) a guarantee for all users, and for all
time, of freedom of navigation in the Suez Canal; (2) co-operation
between the Egyptian authority and the users of the Suez Canal,
with respect for both Egyptian sovereignty and the interests of
Canal users; (3) establishment of a system of tolls and charges
protecting Canal users from exploitation; and (4) provision that

a reasonable percentage of revenues be allocated for Canal improvements.[26]

From 9 to 12 October, the members of the Security Council and Egypt met in private session to explore further the issues in the Suez Canal dispute. When not attending Security Council meetings, Lloyd, Pineau, and Fawzi discussed the matter in the privacy of Hammarskjold's office, with him present as an interested observer. These private talks seemed to make real progress on some of the key issues and may have come close to the basis for a solution. Hammarskjold later dictated from memory a résumé of the meetings in his office. He and Fawzi sensed a curious divergence between Lloyd and Pineau, with Lloyd seeking agreement with Fawzi, and Pineau, aware of the decisions being made in London and Paris, bored with the whole procedure.

Apparently, after some sparring on both sides, the Egyptian position, while rejecting international operation, was quite flexible and forthcoming. Fawzi seems to have indicated that Egypt would:

—accept a system of organized co-operation between a user association and the Egyptian board;
—agree on the allocation of Canal revenues for its development;
—negotiate tolls and charges;
—accept an arbitral tribunal to settle disputes;
—reaffirm the Convention of 1888 and the previous regulations for the administration of the Canal.[27]

At the 12 October meeting, when Lloyd summed up the main points of agreement, Hammarskjold used them as the basis for the six principles (or 'requirements') to govern a solution. These requirements, which became the first section of a revised Anglo-French resolution, were as follows:

(a) There should be free and open transit through the Canal without discrimination, overt or covert—this covers both political and technical aspects;
(b) The sovereignty of Egypt should be respected;
(c) The operation of the Canal should be insulated from the politics of any country;

[26] Ibid., 736th Meeting, 8 Oct. 1956, p. 13, paras. 76, 78–9.
[27] Terence Robertson, *Crisis: The Inside Story of the Suez Conspiracy*, pp. 141–3; Brian Urquhart, *Hammarskjold: The Years of Decision* (Alfred A. Knopf, New York, 1972), pp. 165–8.

(d) The manner of fixing tolls and charges should be decided by agreement between Egypt and the users;

(e) A fair proportion of the dues should be allotted to development;

(f) In case of disputes, unresolved affairs between the Suez Canal Company and the Egyptian Government should be settled by arbitration, with suitable terms of reference and suitable provisions for the payment of sums found to be due.[28]

The parties agreed to continue negotiations in Geneva on 29 October.

London and Paris were not happy with this turn of events; a compromise settlement would clearly not agree with the plans for concerted resort to force (which Pineau may have broached in London on 3 October *en route* to the U.N.). Accordingly, when the Secretary-General reported to a private Security Council session, Lloyd—as directed by Eden—and Pineau stressed the differences from the Eighteen-Power Proposal. And on 13 October, the revised British–French Resolution, besides a first section setting out the agreed six requirements for a solution, included a second section which seemed designed to offend Egypt by ignoring the private talks and the Egyptian concessions. It commended the Eighteen-Power Proposal, noted Egypt's failure to offer 'precise proposals' to meet the requirements, and invited it to do so promptly, urged co-operation between S.C.U.A. and the Egyptian Canal Authority pending a definitive settlement. The Security Council unanimously adopted the first section of the resolution; the second was approved 9 to 2 but was vetoed by the U.S.S.R.[29]

It is not easy to judge whether the dispute might have been settled on the basis of the resolution and private talks. The generality of the agreed 'requirements' left hard questions about their implementation. Apparently the 9–12 October talks explored these topics and suggested practical compromises, reflecting substantial Egyptian concessions. A letter of 24 October from the Secretary-General to Fawzi, which summarized the talks, indicates that ways might have been found to work out most of the practical issues.[30]

The framework for such a settlement would have been organized co-operation between the Egyptian authority operating the Canal and the users' committee, which would have had the right to con-

[28] U.N. SCOR, 11th Year, Supplement for Oct., Nov., and Dec. 1956, Doc. S/3671, 13 Oct. 1956, in *Documents on International Affairs*, p. 249.

[29] Ibid., pp. 249–50; and Doc. S/3675, 13 Oct. 1956, ibid., p. 251.

[30] Doc. S/3728, 24 Oct. 1956, ibid., pp. 254–7.

sult on all matters affecting user interests or rights, with provision for impartial fact-finding, arbitration, and binding awards. Tolls, charges, and allocations for development would have been subject to agreement. Finally, the letter suggested, in case of non-compliance with an award, an aggrieved party 'should be entitled to certain limited "police action", even without recourse to further juridical procedures'. Fawzi replied on 2 November (after the attack), accepting the letter as 'a basis for negotiation', worth trying except for the clause dealing with the right to 'police action'.[31]

In his memoirs, Macmillan states that, while preferring an international agency, Britain was willing to accept Egyptian operation provided a user committee participated 'in the establishment and supervision of Canal policy on tolls, development, patterns of shipping, discrimination and the like; but on the understanding that the Committee could take "automatic" action' if Egypt violated the agreed rules. 'In other words there must be some "teeth" in the plan.'[32] This, of course, was the remedy which Fawzi specifically excluded.

How far was all this shadow-play? The British and French may already have agreed on their collusion with the Israelis; and they certainly had settled it by 16 October at the latest. A Canal solution would have prevented them from going ahead and would have left Nasser in power.[33] Lloyd may have genuinely been seeking a peaceful solution, since he did not favour the use of force and did not learn of the collusion with Israel and France until he returned to London. But others who stressed the Hitler parallel —like Eden and Macmillan—probably had a different view. Nasser's real attitude is also uncertain. Letting Fawzi explore a compromise might have suited his tactical situation, though he may not have intended to follow through. But Egypt could well have been serious, responding to the various pressures already mentioned. And the Fawzi concessions were compatible with the basic refusal to 'give up' operation of the Canal, while offering safeguards consistent with Nasser's earlier assurances.

In any case, Egypt's tactics during the U.N. debates were skilfully devised. First of all, the charge that Britain and France continued to threaten the peace was kept before the world by pub-

---

31 Ibid., pp. 257, 271.
32 Macmillan, p. 144.
33 Kennett Love, Suez: The Twice-Fought War, p. 446.

licizing bellicose statements by their leaders. Second, Egypt maintained a stance of conciliation, stressing its readiness to negotiate or agree regarding specific matters said to threaten Western rights and interests. Third, Egypt relied upon the Soviet Union to block any harmful Security Council resolution, such as the second section of the Anglo-French Resolution of 13 October.[34]

The direct talks among Britain, France, and Egypt, scheduled to continue under the auspices of the Secretary-General in Geneva on 29 October, might have resolved the controversy. Quite clearly, however, Britain and France had other intentions. By mid-October, if not sooner, Mollet and Eden had reached firm agreement that Britain and France would act jointly in concert with Israel against Egypt. The efforts for a peaceful solution, whether serious or a pretence, were at an end.

[34] Department of State Press Release 543, 16 Oct. 1956, in Department of State, *Middle East*, p. 127; D. C. Watt, *Documents on the Suez Crisis*, pp. 62–4; U.N. SCOR, 11th Year, Supplement for Oct., Nov., and Dec. 1956, Doc. S/3675, in Department of State, *Middle East*, p. 120.

IV

RESORT TO FORCE

In the second phase of the Suez crisis, the Israeli attack and the Anglo-French intervention raised directly the issue of the relation of law and the U.N. to the actual use of force.

1. FRENCH–BRITISH–ISRAELI COLLUSION

From the start of the crisis, Britain and France had begun to plan and prepare for possible military action, as Eden advised Eisenhower on 27 July. To unseat Nasser or cut him down to size would probably require a resort to force. The critical question was when to strike and under what conditions. In part, the answer was determined by military factors. Neither Britain nor France had the military means to react forcibly against Egypt immediately after the Canal seizure. To organize and mount effective military measures would require six weeks or more. That period, therefore, was available for 'peaceful efforts' without delaying preparations for military action.[1]

Indeed, the search for a peaceful solution was a political precondition to force, at least for Britain, as Eden recognized. At home the Labour Party and public opinion would demand it, including ultimate appeal to the U.N. The U.S. attitude also made that effort a practical necessity. Since military action might block the Canal and direct access to Middle East oil, as well as provoke Soviet threats, U.S. support might be crucial to avoid a disaster. Hence Britain felt compelled to placate U.S. insistence on a negotiated solution enough to ensure at least its acquiescence in ultimate resort to force. And France, though less vulnerable and constrained, wanted British collaboration.

British–French military planning had to contend with supply shortages, logistics difficulties, joint command, and above all, political ambiguity and vacillation. By 18 August, the joint French–British team had obtained approval of an operation, to be known as 'Musketeer', which involved an assault on Alexandria

[1] Eden, pp. 476–80.

in mid-September, starting with air attacks, and with landings two days later. To allow the action to be adjusted to the political situation, the schedule called for decisions, on whether to proceed, to be made in principle fifteen days before the action (2 September) and definitely a week before (10 September). The First London Conference and the Menzies mission fell within the period needed for military preparations. But the S.C.U.A. conference and the delayed U.N. appeal clearly involved successive postponements of the military action. On 2 September, the planned assault was delayed eight days to 25 September, and on 8 September it was put off again to 1 October, with a basic change in the whole concept. The target was now to be Port Said, and any landings were to be preceded by eight to ten days of 'aeropsychological' attacks to break the Egyptian will. On 19 September, and then on 1 October, the starting date was again deferred.[2]

The original planning did not involve Israel, which had its own reasons for hostility to Nasser. For eight years Egypt had maintained an economic blockade and denied Israeli ships or cargoes the use of the Suez Canal, and for nearly as long it had blocked the access to Israel's port at Eilat by closing the Straits of Tiran. These actions were hurting Israel's economy by forcing her to use the long route around the Cape to reach East Africa or Asia. Moreover, raids and reprisals between Israel and its Arab neighbours, especially Egypt, had gone on despite the 1949 armistice. After the Gaza Raid of February 1955, Nasser organized the fedayeen, based in Gaza and Sinai, to step up such raids, which were especially active in the summer of 1955 and spring of 1956. They took a steady toll despite harsh Israeli reprisals. And all along, Nasser and other Arab leaders continued to claim 'belligerency' and the ultimate intent to destroy Israel. The massive rearming of the Egyptian army, starting with the Soviet arms deal of September 1955, created a growing Israeli fear of attack.

Israel had repeatedly denounced the closing of the Suez Canal and the Gulf of Aqaba as illegal.[3] It claimed the right to use the

[2] The best account so far of this aspect is André Beaufre, *The Suez Expedition: 1956* (Praeger, New York, 1969), largely relied on here. For a British account, see A. J. Barker, *Suez: The Seven Day War* (Faber and Faber, London, 1964).

[3] For a discussion of the legal issues involved in the blockades, see R. R. Baxter, *The Law of International Waterways* (Harvard University Press, Cambridge, Mass., 1964), pp. 221-36, 160-3, and 209-16. See also Louis M. Bloomfield, *Egypt, Israel and the Gulf of Aqaba in International Law* (Carswell,

Canal under the 1888 Convention, and the Gulf under general international law, and asserted that the armistice ended any rights of belligerency for Egypt. Moreover, in 1951, the Security Council had sustained the Israeli claims explicitly as to the Canal and by implication as to Aqaba, and had directed Egypt to cease its interference. Yet this action was not enforced in any way: Egypt had totally ignored it, continuing to impose its restrictions on Israeli and neutral shipping. In 1954, Israel's efforts to get relief from the Security Council were vetoed by the Soviet Union, and Egypt confiscated an Israeli vessel which had sought to use the Canal. Similarly, Israel had not succeeded in obtaining any stoppage of the fedayeen raids through the U.N. or the Truce Commission.

By October 1955, Ben-Gurion began to contemplate war against Nasser. He directed Moshe Dayan, his Chief of Staff, to prepare plans for a Sinai campaign, In November 1955, on taking over again as Prime Minister, Ben-Gurion's policy speech stressed security and especially the threat from Egypt with its Soviet arms. Referring to the various hostile actions, he warned: 'This unilateral warfare must cease, for it cannot remain unilateral indefinitely', and, 'If our rights are affected by acts of violence on land or sea, we shall reserve freedom of action to defend them in the most effective manner.'[4]

Israel had also stepped up its efforts to obtain armaments, particularly from France. For over a year before the attack, France had been secretly supplying arms to Israel well in excess of the agreed scale under the Tripartite Declaration of 1950. Israeli airforce pilots were being brought to France in civilian clothes and trained to fly and fight the French Mystère jets. French instructors also began to appear in Israel. The initial French motive, according to Mollet, who became Prime Minister in early 1956, was to assist a small, courageous, democratic nation threatened by aggressive neighbours, especially Nasser, who, as it happened, was also helping to fuel the Algerian revolt. Mollet sharply stepped up the supply of armaments, which arrived secretly and in quantity, starting in July 1956, and continuing to the end of September. In a major speech to the Knesset on 15 October 1956, Ben-Gurion an-

---

Toronto, 1957); and Thomas T. Huang, 'Some International and Legal Aspects of the Suez Canal Problem', Am. J. Int'l., vol. 51, no. 2 (Apr. 1957), pp. 277–307.

[4] David Ben-Gurion, *Israel: A Personal History* (Funk & Wagnalls, Inc., New York, 1971), pp. 446–50.

nounced the rearming of Israel and laid the foundation for the attack two weeks later. He reviewed the hostile Arab actions and threats against Israel, denounced them as violations of the Charter, and stressed the failure of the U.N. to provide any remedies. He specifically stated that, under Article 51 of the U.N. Charter, Israel had the inherent right to self-defence against the fedayeen raids, and he warned that continuation of Nasser's 'arbitrary blockade' of the Suez Canal and Red Sea straits would 'disturb the stability of the peace in the Middle East'.[5]

By that time, of course, Israel and France and Britain were planning their collusion. It developed by stages, starting with French feelers perhaps as early as August. In the early stages, two key figures were the French Defence Minister, Maurice Bourges-Maunoury, and Shimon Peres, of the Israel Defence Ministry, who had been working for several years to get French arms. In seeking French arms support during 1955, Peres had got to know Bourges-Maunoury, who was then Interior Minister and in charge of Algerian affairs. Starting in August 1956, or earlier, the arms supply talks offered an easy context for informal exchanges about the possibilities of an Israeli attack on Sinai and the British–French military planning regarding Suez. France and Israel each had its own objectives, but their common enemy was Nasser.[6]

The idea of a joint action was tempting: Israel could attack Sinai to destroy the fedayeen bases and to open the Gulf of Aqaba while the French and British could focus on the Canal. As Dayan and others saw it, the potential British–French military action presented a golden opportunity for Israel. For a preventive attack on Egyptian bases in Gaza and Sinai, Israel needed air and naval support, which France and Britain could furnish. Collusion with Israel appealed to the French leaders, frustrated by British hesitation. Its political costs in the Middle East were tolerable since Algeria had already eroded French standing among the Arabs. And at home, such joint military action would be supported from the Right (concerned about Algeria) and from the Left (committed to Israel).

During September, French–Israeli planning went on, mainly among the military and defence staffs. The Israeli concept was

---

[5] Ibid., pp. 496–502.

[6] Michael Bar-Zohar, *Ben Gurion: The Armed Prophet*, pp. 197, 205; Shimon Peres, *David's Sling* (Weidenfeld and Nicolson, London, 1970), p. 56; Moshe Dayan, *Diary of the Sinai Campaign* (Schocken Books, New York, 1967), p. 25.

tailored to its national needs. (1) French (and, it was hoped, British) air support would protect Israel's cities and immobilize, and if possible destroy, the Egyptian air force. (2) The threat of U.K.–French attack at the Canal would pin down most of the Egyptian ground forces there, so as to give Israeli ground forces a three-to-one superiority in the Sinai peninsula. On these premisses, the French–Israeli military staff worked out plans on which agreement was reached by 10 October.[7]

The British were drawn in during this stage. Mollet was most reluctant to move without Britain, and Ben-Gurion also wanted the British involved. He believed that although French planes could provide fighter cover, the longer-range British Canberra bombers were needed to strike the Egyptian airfields and their Ilyushin-28 bombers. In addition, he feared that France might back out if Britain did not take part, and that if the British were not committed, they might turn on Israel to placate the Arabs. Yet Britain was bound to be hesitant and cautious about collusion with Israel. Nasser's enemies in the Middle East might condone a direct British–French attack on him, but they could hardly forgive Britain for joining forces with Israel. Thus, if overt, such collaboration could hardly bolster Britain's position in the region. Politically, Eden was also becoming increasingly vulnerable: Labour was now definitely opposed to force; and Britain was more concerned with U.S. attitudes than was France.[8]

The decision for a concerted attack was apparently reached by stages. After the S.C.U.A. episode, Eden became more and more exasperated with the United States, and especially with Dulles. He feared that passage of time would defuse the crisis, especially as the Canal continued to operate normally even after the European pilots were withdrawn on 15 September. In late September the Israelis and French canvassed the situation fully; shortly afterwards, Pineau flew to London. At this time Eden may have agreed informally to France's acting as intermediary between the two allies and Israel, possibly to explore military co-operation.

On 2 October, Dulles again annoyed the British. In a press conference, he admitted differences in approach to the Canal problem and other issues, such as colonialism, where 'the United States plays a somewhat independent role'. Its role 'will be to try to aid that process [from colonialism to independence] without identify-

---

[7] André Beaufre, *The Suez Expedition: 1956*, pp. 69–78.
[8] Bar-Zohar and Kimche interviews, in Moncrieff, pp. 90–2.

ing itself 100 per cent either with the colonial powers or with the powers which are primarily and uniquely concerned with the problem of getting their independence as rapidly as possible'. The British and French governments were bitter. *The Times* of London was quick to accuse Dulles of 'gross misrepresentation' and 'grave disservice to Anglo-American unity'.[9]

The U.N. proceedings were also troubling the British. Dulles's readiness to examine means for safeguarding user rights other than international control, as well as the private talks in October, raised the spectre of a potential settlement based on Egyptian operation with user supervision or co-operation. Any such alternative would clearly not discredit Nasser but would certainly foreclose resort to force.

The British decision also was based on a serious political misjudgement, as Macmillan makes clear in his memoirs. Relying on wartime friendships, indecision, and the imminent U.S. election on 6 November (with its important Jewish vote), Eden, Macmillan, and their colleagues were apparently confident that Eisenhower would acquiesce, or merely dissociate the U.S., if the British and French faced him with a *fait accompli*. Ben-Gurion may well have made a similar miscalculation. To their serious mistake was added another about the assault itself. Apparently, the British leaders expected that extended 'aeropsychological' bombing would panic the Egyptians into overthrowing Nasser, even without a physical takeover.[10]

By mid-October then, whatever the earlier informal soundings, the British were ready to commit themselves explicitly to the French–Israeli plans for concerted attack. On 14 October, a visit by General Maurice Challe to Eden brought the issue to a head. To satisfy Eden's concern about collaboration with Israel, the plans were based on the 'peacekeeping' pretext. After consulting with key ministers, Eden on 16 October flew to France to meet with Mollet. They agreed on plans and roles in the coming Israeli attack on Egypt on 29 October. In anticipation, Ben-Gurion had made a major speech on 15 October, setting out the violations of Israel's rights and the failure of the U.N. or others to provide a remedy. Yet the co-operation was nearly upset when Israel launched a severe raid against Jordan, which at once appealed for help from its British ally, from Nasser, and from Iran. This

[9] Department of State, pp. 103–4; *The Times* (London), 6 Oct. 1956.
[10] Macmillan, p. 149; and cf. Eisenhower, p. 56. Beaufre, pp. 54–6, 138.

confused contretemps was, however, brought under control before it disrupted the Sinai–Suez operation. The victory of the pro-Nasser faction in the Jordanian election led promptly to Jordan's joining an alliance with Egypt and Syria.[11]

Meanwhile, the U.S.S.R. was becoming preoccupied by eruptions in Eastern Europe. On 19 October, the Poles removed the Soviet Marshal who was their Defence Minister, rehabilitated Gomulka, and defied Khrushchev's threats to suppress the upheaval by force. And on 22 October, the Hungarians revolted and forced the restoration of Imre Nagy as Premier. The continuing disorders and ultimate Soviet suppression paralleled in time the unfolding of the Middle East crisis and enabled the British, French, and Israelis to discount the Soviet threats to intervene or assist Egypt.

To formalize the collusion plans and reassure Ben-Gurion, France, Israel, and Britain held a secret meeting in Sèvres from 22 to 24 October. Those attending included Ben-Gurion, Dayan, and Peres, Mollet, Pineau, and Bourges-Maunoury, Lloyd and Patrick Dean. The outcome was a secret three-power agreement setting out the timetable and moves in the concerted attacks by Israel, Britain, and France. Israel was to attack on 29 October and to seem to threaten the Canal. The British and French, acting ostensibly to protect the Canal and separate the combatants, would issue an ultimatum calling on Israel and Egypt to withdraw ten miles from the Canal and on Egypt to accept temporary U.K.–French occupation of Canal sites. The rejection of the ultimatum by Egypt would provide the pretext for Britain to bomb Egypt and destroy its air force. France would furnish air cover and coastal security for Israel as well as veto any resolution in the Security Council that would label it an aggressor. Britain and France would commence to land forces on 6 November—the day of the U.S. elections.[12]

Thereafter, events moved rapidly. On 25 October the intervention plan was approved by the British Cabinet, seemingly without major objection—one dissenter, Sir Walter Monckton, having resigned two weeks before as Defence Minister. The same day, Israel began to mobilize her armed forces, while her ambassador,

---

[11] Ben-Gurion, pp. 496–502; Peres, pp. 189–99; Anthony Nutting, *No End of a Lesson: The Story of Suez*, pp. 93–4.

[12] Terence Robertson, *Crisis: The Inside Story of the Suez Conspiracy*, pp. 155–62; Nutting, pp. 104–5; Pineau interview in Moncrieff, pp. 93–5; Terence Robertson interview in Moncrieff, pp. 98–100.

Abba Eban, was assuring the Security Council that Israel would never start a war against her Arab neighbours and was also denouncing Egypt for organizing fedayeen gangs to cross Israeli borders from Jordan and the Gaza Strip. This was to be Israel's formal ground for the attack.

The United States, which had been expressing optimism about prospects in the Middle East, became concerned at the 'blackout' of allied contact and the reports of Israeli mobilization. On 27 October, Eisenhower sent a strong warning to Ben-Gurion against taking any 'forceful initiative in the Middle East'. Next day, the President, perhaps hoping to give pause to the British and French as well as the Israelis, made passing mention of the Tripartite Declaration which pledged the three allies to take action to prevent violations of frontiers or armistice lines in the Middle East.[13]

On 29 October, Israel dropped paratroops at the Mitla Pass, forty miles from the Suez Canal, and followed up with a military thrust into the Sinai Peninsula of Egypt. A statement issued by the Israeli Ministry of Foreign Affairs said, 'Israel has taken the necessary measures to destroy the Egyptian fedayeen bases in the Sinai Peninsula.'[14]

Dulles at once saw the attack as extremely serious: 'The Canal is likely to be disrupted and the oil pipelines through the Middle East broken. If these things happen, we must expect British and French intervention. In fact, they appeared to be ready for it and may even have concerted their action with the Israelis.' The United States asked for an immediate meeting of the Security Council. Before the Council could act, however—on 30 October—the British and French issued their ultimatum to Israel and Egypt to lay the foundation for their intervention.[15]

---

[13] Michael Adams, *Suez and After: Year of Crisis* (Beacon Press, Boston, 1958), p. 81; see also Kennett Love, *Suez: The Twice-Fought War*, p. 474.

[14] For a description of the military operations, see Beaufre; Shlomo Barer, *The Weekend War* (Yoseloff, New York, 1960); Samuel L. A. Marshall, *Sinai Victory* (Morrow, New York, 1958); Dayan; Robert D. Q. Henriques, *A Hundred Hours to Suez* (Viking Press, New York, 1957); Department of State, *Middle East*, p. 135 (source of quotation).

[15] Quoted in Eisenhower, p. 73. For divergent legal analyses of the Anglo-French right of intervention, see Quincy Wright, 'Intervention, 1956', Am. J. Int'l L., vol. 51, no. 2 (Apr. 1957), p. 272; and Arthur Goodhart and Quincy Wright, 'Some Legal Aspects of the Suez Situation', in P. W. Thayer (ed.), *Tensions in the Middle East* (Johns Hopkins Press, Baltimore, Md., 1958), pp. 243-72.

2. THE UNITED STATES POSITION

The U.S. attitude and actions, expressed through the U.N. and outside, were decisive in the aftermath of the attack. The whole affair was extremely painful for both Eisenhower and Dulles. Both were distressed at having to oppose and coerce the closest U.S. allies as well as Israel. Yet they were not deflected from demanding compliance with their interpretations of the U.N. obligation to refrain from the use of force under these conditions. From the start, of course, the U.S. had consistently counselled, in public and private, against resorting to force except as an inescapable last resort.

The divergence in outlook between the U.S. and its two allies was profound. The allies were focusing almost entirely on the costs of *not* destroying Nasser as a threat to their positions in the Middle East. The U.S. assessed the Canal dispute and the stakes mainly in relation to its efforts to build world stability and order and to contain Soviet expansion. The attack on Egypt affected those efforts in various ways:

1. Having seen the devastating consequences of war, Eisenhower was seriously committed to strengthening and supporting the U.N. as an important instrument for stable peace. And Dulles shared this view. In a September press conference, Eisenhower said, for example: 'I think this: We established the United Nations to abolish aggression, and I am not going to be a party to aggression if it is humanly possible to avoid it or I can detect it before it occurs.' For both of them, the lesson of the League of Nations was a vivid warning that failure to resist resort to force would undermine the U.N. On television on 31 October, the President explained his policy: 'We believe these actions to have been taken in error. For we do not accept the use of force as a wise and proper instrument for settlement of international disputes.'[16]

He hoped that the U.N. General Assembly would be able to end the conflict. There 'the opinion of the world can be brought to bear in our quest for a just end to this tormenting problem ... I am ever more deeply convinced that the processes of the United Nations represent the soundest hope for peace in the world.' Later, when seeking Congressional support for sanctions to force Israeli withdrawal, 'Eisenhower stated flatly that he did not know how to protect American interests in the Middle East except through the

16 *Documents on International Affairs*, p. 204 (1st quotation); Department of State, *Middle East*, pp. 148–51 (2nd quotation on p. 149).

United Nations. If the United States failed to support the United Nations on the Israel issue ... it would be a lethal blow to the principles of the world peace organization.'[17]

The U.N.'s inability to halt Soviet intervention in Hungary was already damaging its standing. An added failure to cope with the Suez attack in violation of the Charter could discredit it utterly. In his first General Assembly speech, Dulles stressed the danger: if the principle of renunciation of force as a method of settling disputes is no longer respected, if a nation subject to injustice has the right to resort to force to correct that injustice, the U.N. Charter would be torn to shreds and the world would again be a world of anarchy.[18]

2. To Eisenhower and Dulles, the British–French action and purposes were reminiscent of the imperial past and of Western efforts to impose its will on weaker peoples. Such an approach was wholly out of keeping with post-war conditions and the strong new nationalism of the less developed world. The United States, and its allies, could not afford to be stigmatized as seeking to prolong an outmoded 'colonial' era of imposed domination. In urging the British to agree in 1954 to withdraw from Egypt, Eisenhower later wrote: 'I believed that it would be undesirable and impractical for the British to retain sizable forces permanently in a territory of a jealous and resentful government and an openly hostile population.' The U.S. stance was anti-colonial to some degree, therefore, although this embarrassed its allies. Even if the Suez attack succeeded in discrediting Nasser, the long-range damage to Western influence in Africa, Asia, and Latin America would be far too costly. Thus, the U.S. felt impelled to separate itself sharply and clearly from the British–French action.[19]

Accordingly, the U.S. took the lead in seeking U.N. action against both the Israeli attack and the British–French ultimatum. In the Security Council, the U.S. resolution called on Israel to leave Egypt without delay and asked all member states to 'refrain from the use of force or the threat of force' and 'from giving any military, economic, or financial assistance to Israel so long as it has not complied with this resolution'. The allied split was dramatized by the British and French veto.

[17] Department of State, *Middle East*, p. 150 (1st quotation); Sherman Adams, *Firsthand Report* (Harper & Brothers, New York, 1961), p. 282 (2nd quotation).
[18] Department of State, *Middle East*, pp. 151–7 (especially p. 153).
[19] Eisenhower, p. 23.

3. The U.S. was greatly concerned with preventing the Soviet Union from capitalizing on the attack. It was, of course, a windfall for the U.S.S.R. in diverting attention from its aggression against Hungary. But beyond that, the U.S. feared that the U.S.S.R. could exploit the attack to enhance its influence in the Middle East. As Eisenhower wrote in his memoirs, 'We could not permit the Soviet Union to seize the leadership in the struggle against the use of force in the Middle East and thus win the confidence of the new independent nations of the world.' At the outset of the crisis, the Soviets offered 'volunteers' to Egypt to help repulse the expected Anglo-French invasion. On 5 November, Bulganin wrote strongly worded messages to Eden, Mollet, and Ben-Gurion condemning their 'aggressive war in Egypt', warning of the potential 'dangerous consequences', and also mentioning the 'capabilities of Soviet missiles'. In a note to President Eisenhower he proposed 'close co-operation' to stop the 'aggression against the Egyptian people' by joint use of their armed forces.[20]

The U.S. responded in two ways to forestall any Soviet involvement. First, it warned that direct Soviet interference would be met by a U.S. reaction. Second, the U.S. sought to internationalize the handling of the crisis under U.N. auspices, and to play down unilateral steps by the U.S. or U.S.S.R. The Canadian proposal for the creation of a United Nations Emergency Force to supervise a ceasefire and separate the belligerents fitted perfectly into this pattern. Made up of troops from smaller powers, such a force would remove any pretext for Soviet 'volunteers'.[21]

4. Another objective in regard to the Soviet Union was to avoid any direct confrontation which could escalate into nuclear war. While the Soviet threats were viewed as primarily propaganda, if they should lead to any direct conflict the consequences would fall mainly on the U.S., rather than the U.K. or France. As Dulles saw it, 'America would have to pay the piper; America must call the tune'.[22]

5. The United States could not condone the use of force for other reasons related to its global role. At the moment when Anglo-French and Israeli forces were fighting in Egypt, Soviet forces were quelling the last vestiges of resistance in Hungary. To

20 Ibid., p. 83. Department of State, *Middle East*, pp. 183–7, 180–1.
21 Department of State, *Middle East*, pp. 182–3.
22 Richard Goold-Adams, *The Time of Power: A Reappraisal of John Foster Dulles* (Weidenfeld and Nicolson, London, 1962), p. 216.

justify Anglo-French action would make it much harder to condemn the Soviet aggression. The United States also had to consider the impact of this use of force as a precedent for its other
allies who had serious grievances. How could Dulles discourage
Chiang Kai-shek's and Syngman Rhee's desire to solve their problems by force if the United States approved the use of force by its
other allies? The interest of the United States in promoting stability and restraint in these and other areas made it vital to oppose
force at Suez.

6. Finally, on the practical plane, Eisenhower was convinced that
the British–French attack would not solve the Canal issue. Even
if the two powers captured the Canal, they could not operate it
over Egyptian resistance. Lives would be lost, commerce disrupted,
and all the costs suffered without any benefits.

Eisenhower wrote:

Experiences in India, Indochina, and Algeria, too, demonstrated that
since the founding of the United Nations in 1945, the use of occupying
troops in foreign territories to sustain a policy was a costly and difficult
business. Unless the occupying power was ready to employ the brutalities
of dictatorship, local unrest would soon grow into guerrilla resistance,
then open revolt, and possibly, wide-scale conflict.

The U.S. wished to stop the Anglo-French intervention because
it could only lead to disaster.[23]

For all these reasons, Eisenhower and Dulles were determined to
halt and reverse the British–French–Israeli attack and vigorously
to apply economic and political leverage to that end. The blockage
of the Canal, the disruption of oil shipments and other commerce,
as well as the invasion, put severe strains on the limited British
monetary reserves. As the Chancellor of the Exchequer, Harold
Macmillan, commented, the strain was greater than the economy
could bear. A U.S. loan to ease this pressure was made conditional
on a British and French ceasefire. Later, the U.S. again used its
economic strength in pressing for the removal of the Anglo-French
invasion force. Meanwhile, the run on sterling was continuing. In
the month of November, Britain lost $279 million from its total
gold and dollar reserves. The need for U.S. assistance for the
pound and for oil was too great to resist.[24]

[23] Eisenhower, p. 40.
[24] N.Y. Times, 5 Nov. 1956; Macmillan, pp. 161–9; Robertson, p. 264; Eden,
pp. 622–4; N.Y. Times, 7 Dec. 1956.

Inevitably, France, Israel, and especially Britain bitterly resented the U.S. course. The President was caught in a squeeze. He wished to preserve the Western alliance and the friendships dating back to the Second World War. Yet he was convinced that failure to oppose the use of force would ruin the United Nations, drive the Arab States to the Soviets, and seriously harm U.S. interests in other areas of the world. Therefore he sought to tread a narrow path. He insisted throughout on his deep friendship for Britain, France, and Israel, and his regret at having to oppose their ill-advised actions. As early as 31 October, when the Anglo-French ultimatum was issued, the President in his television address said that the 'error' of Britain, France, and Israel did not 'minimize' the U.S. friendship for them. On 5 November 1956, when an aide talked to him of halting oil supplies to Britain and France, Eisenhower said, 'Good lands! I'm a friend of theirs. I'm not going to make life too complicated for them.' When Eden telephoned from London after the election to arrange to come to Washington, 'Eisenhower greeted the Prime Minister with the warmth of one old friend getting together with another.' While at first receptive to Eden's idea, Eisenhower finally refused after the State Department persuaded him that such a visit would be misinterpreted. On 7 December, however, when the House of Commons endorsed the withdrawal of British forces from the Port Said area, the United States announced that it would take steps to aid Britain in meeting its financial crisis.[25]

In short, the President sought to pursue a consistent course throughout the crisis in support of the principles of the U.N. as he understood them. That support was not merely verbal; it included severe pressure on allied states led by personal friends. And the course was adopted before the election in the face of potentially high political costs. Doubtless, Eisenhower acted from a complex set of reasons; yet a major factor was a genuine commitment to U.N. principles, although reinforced in this case by other interests and practical judgements. Even so, this course entailed the painful necessity to oppose the closest allies of the United States and to divide the Atlantic Alliance, which embodied security interests of high priority in the midst of the Cold War.

[25] N.Y. Times, 1 Nov. 1956; Love, p. 623 (1st quotation); Herman Finer, Dulles Over Suez: The Theory and Practice of his Diplomacy, pp. 372 (2nd quotation), 456; Sherman Adams, Firsthand Report, pp. 259-70 (3rd quotation on p. 259).

3. FROM INVASION TO CEASEFIRE

On the morning of 30 October 1956, the United Nations began the difficult process of applying the principles of the Charter to the Suez Crisis. At the request of the United States, the Security Council met in emergency session to consider the Israeli attack into Gaza and the Sinai Peninsula, begun the night before. The U.S. draft resolution focused entirely on the obligation to refrain from the resort to force. It called for immediate withdrawal of Israeli forces from Egypt and urged all states to refrain from intervening with the use of force or threat of its use. During the debate, word came that the United Kingdom and France had issued a joint ultimatum to both Egypt and Israel to cease all warlike action and withdraw all forces to positions ten miles from the Canal. Furthermore, the government of Egypt was requested to accede 'to the temporary occupation by Anglo-French forces of key positions at Port Said, Ismailia, and Suez'. The ultimatum was due to expire at 6.00 a.m., Egyptian time, 31 October. The threat of reaction in the event of non-compliance was most explicit: 'If at the expiration of that time one or both Governments have not undertaken to comply with the above requirements, United Kingdom and French forces will intervene in whatever strength may be necessary to secure compliance.'[26] The Council recessed until afternoon.

Israel and the U.K. and France took very different lines in justifying resort to force. Israel sought to bring its action within the terms of the Charter, specifically as an exercise of the inherent right to self-defence under Article 51. Accordingly, it defined the purpose of its Sinai operation solely as the removal of the Egyptian bases for the fedayeen attacks on Israel, which imperilled its security. The blockade of the Canal and Aqaba was mentioned only as evidence of Nasser's basic hostility. In his long speech, Eban (1) quoted Egyptian official statements identifying the fedayeen as organized and supported by Egypt; (2) detailed the fedayeen raids and Israeli casualties since April 1956; (3) argued that the fedayeen were a new means for waging war to destroy Israel; (4) condemned the failure of the U.N. to provide a remedy; (5) denounced Egypt's claim of continuing belligerency to justify its hostile acts; and (6) invoked Israel's 'sovereign rights of

---

[26] U.N. SCOR, 11th Year, Supplement for Oct., Nov., and Dec. 1956, Doc. S/3710, 30 Oct. 1956, p. 110; ibid., 11th Year, 749th Meeting, 30 Oct. 1956, pp. 6, 4 (source of quotations).

self-defence' for the sole purpose of wiping out the fedayeen bases in Sinai. Egypt's delegate dismissed the Israeli arguments as irrelevant to the agenda item. And no other delegate (except the French) endorsed the Israeli position.[27]

In Britain, Eden and his Cabinet justified the intervention to Parliament as an exercise of the inherent right to protect nationals and their property from imminent danger, broadly within the ambit of Article 51. In the U.N. Sir Pierson Dixon defended the attack primarily as a 'police action' to separate the belligerents and safeguard the Canal. He insisted that occupation of key Canal positions was a necessary temporary expedient.

For the moment [he said] there is no action that the Security Council can constructively take which would contribute to the twin objectives of stopping the fighting and safeguarding free passage through the Suez Canal ... in the circumstances nothing would be gained by pressing on with the consideration of the United States draft resolution.[28]

The Council was not able to act with the requisite speed and decision, he said, and should therefore refrain from any action until both belligerents had responded to the Anglo-French ultimatum.

If we felt that the Security Council could in fact at this moment separate the parties and protect the Canal, of course we would rather proceed in that way ... we feel grave doubt whether in fact action could be taken by this Council with sufficient speed. Events are moving too fast, too fast for words even from this Council to have the right effect.[29]

While adopting this line, the French delegate also supported Israel; but he attacked Nasser in far broader terms than Eban had done. Citing Mollet and Pineau, he denounced Nasser's boundless ambition as a grave menace:

[His] aims, aims fundamentally incompatible with the United Nations Charter, are openly affirmed, namely, the annihilation of the State of Israel, the expansion of Egyptian imperialism from the Atlantic to the Persian Gulf, open intervention in French international affairs, direct material assistance to rebellious citizens, and the seizure, in defiance of all treaties and rules of international law, of a waterway which is essential to the life of the nations.[30]

The U.N., he urged, should take no action until Egypt and Israel had replied to the ultimatum.

[27] Ibid., 11th Year, 749th Meeting, 30 Oct. 1956, pp. 8–19.
[28] Ibid., pp. 3–4.   [29] Ibid., p. 24.
[30] Ibid., pp. 26–30 (quotation on p. 29).

In the House of Commons the next day, Eden pressed the broader attack: the Egyptians were to blame for what was happening. They had created an 'explosive situation in the Middle East' by their actions. They had made clear over and over

their intention to destroy Israel, just as they have made plain that they would drive the Western Powers out of the Middle East. It is really not tolerable that the greatest sea highway in the world, one on which our Western life so largely depends, should be subject to the [resulting] dangers.[31]

The United States draft resolution, supported 7 to 2, with 2 abstentions, was vetoed by Britain and France lest any United Nations response deprive them of the justification for their intervention. In the eyes of most delegations, the United Nations was the proper locus for settlement attempts. Upon learning of the Anglo-French ultimatum, President Eisenhower immediately informed Prime Ministers Eden and Mollet in most forceful terms of his hope that the United Nations would be permitted to settle the controversy by peaceful means without the further complication of Anglo-French armed intervention.

Indeed, any 'temporary' imposition of Anglo-French troops, by force if necessary, to 'protect' the Suez Canal appeared entirely unjustified, even in practical terms. At the time the ultimatum was issued, the fighting was about one hundred miles east of the Canal, and the only Egyptian troops were in the vicinity of the waterway itself. Thus, the ultimatum was an open invitation to the Israeli forces to continue towards the specified line ten miles east of the Canal, while Egypt was ordered to abandon the entire Sinai Peninsula to advancing Israeli forces. As the deadline neared, Israeli forces were still not within ten miles of the Canal; and, according to an Egyptian report, the flow of traffic through the Suez Canal was smooth, as yet unimpeded by the hostilities in the Sinai Desert. Despite denials, the obvious Israeli bias of the ultimatum led many delegates to suspect Anglo-French collusion with Israel.

After Egypt had rejected the stationing of British and French troops at the Canal, the bombing of towns along the Suez Canal began on 31 October. Both the U.S.S.R. and the U.S. condemned the action against Egypt. Hammarskjold, initially stunned, was

[31] Great Britain, H.C. Deb., vol. 558, 31 Oct. 1956, p. 1446.

categorical in rejecting the Anglo-French argument. He was torn between his duty to remain impartial and his duty to defend the principles of the Charter. That afternoon he said:

As a servant of the Organization, the Secretary-General has the duty to maintain his usefulness by avoiding public stands on conflicts between member Nations unless and until such an action might help resolve the conflict. However, the discretion and impartiality thus imposed on the Secretary-General by the character of his immediate task, may not degenerate into a policy of expediency. He must also be a servant of the principles of the Charter, and its aims must ultimately determine what for him is right and wrong. For that he must stand ... Were the members to consider that another view of the duties of the Secretary-General than the one here stated would better serve the interest of the Organization, it is their obvious right to act accordingly.[32]

Most of the Council members, including the two invading powers, responded by affirming complete confidence in his impartiality and integrity.

Unable to act with Britain and France opposing, the Council decided to transfer the matter to an emergency special session of the General Assembly under the Uniting for Peace Resolution. The terms of reference for the General Assembly were vague, affording wide latitude to expand its handling of the crisis beyond the military actions of Israel, Great Britain, and France. The General Assembly was acutely aware that ending hostilities would not cure the turmoil in the Middle East unless the underlying political causes were resolved. From the outset, the Assembly was urged by some to consider the many-faceted problem in its full complexity, including the issues of ceasefire, withdrawal, and solution of the underlying political disputes that had precipitated the Israeli attempt to obtain redress unilaterally. The simpler course was to condemn the aggressors and call upon them to withdraw all forces from Egyptian territory. This coincided with the demands of Egypt, her Arab neighbours, and India. But, as the Chinese delegate pointed out, a ceasefire and withdrawal, while essential, were not a sufficient response. 'We want to stop the war; at the same time we must work hard to remove the cause of war.'[33]

[32] U.N. SCOR, 11th Year, 751st Meeting, 31 Oct. 1956, p. 1.
[33] Ibid., p. 12; U.N. GAOR, 11th Session, Plenary Meetings and Annexes, First Emergency Special Session, Plenary Meeting 561, 1 Nov. 1956, p. 8 (source of quotation).

The crucial question was the relation between ending hostilities and the solution of the underlying issues. The United States gave its answer in a television address by the President on 31 October, elaborated in Dulles's statement to the General Assembly on the evening of 1 November. The U.S. recognized that in resorting to force, Israel, Britain, and France were reacting to serious provocations by Egypt. 'We are not blind to the fact', Dulles said, 'that what has happened within the last two or three days has emerged from a murky background.' He was most emphatic in adding that 'these provocations—serious as they were—cannot justify the resort to armed force which has occurred during these last two or three days and which is continuing tonight.'[34] It was generally recognized that the United Nations had been at fault in failing to relieve the outstanding sources of tension in the Middle East. More should be done soon to deal with the many injustices in the Middle East situation. But to accept that whenever a nation felt itself subject to injustice it had a right to resort to force would destroy the U.N. and create anarchy. Great efforts had been made to resolve the Suez Canal dispute by peaceful means, and the October negotiations opened the prospect that a just and acceptable solution could be found soon. Certainly, peaceful processes had not been exhausted. The armed attack by the three members was a grave error, contrary to U.N. principles and purposes.

The draft U.S. resolution (adopted on 2 November) called for: (1) an immediate ceasefire, halting of bringing in forces, and withdrawal of all forces behind armistice lines; (2) refraining from raids across armistice lines; (3) scrupulous observation of the armistice agreements; (4) refraining from any actions delaying these steps; (5) following upon a ceasefire, measures to reopen the Canal and restore freedom of passage. Although concern with the incursions was expressed in the resolution, it refrained from fixing the blame on any state or states.

Dulles admitted that his resolution was only a first step, and that the United Nations was obliged to do more than merely restore the conditions out of which the tragedy confronting the Assembly had arisen:

Peace is a coin which has two sides—one is the avoidance of the use of force and the other is the creation of conditions of justice. In the long run you cannot expect one without the other.... There needs to be

[34] Ibid., p. 10.

something better than the uneasy armistices which have existed now for these eight years between Israel and its Arab neighbors.

But the first thing, Dulles argued, was to stop the fighting promptly. 'Then we shall turn with renewed vigour to curing the injustices out of which this trouble has arisen.' The Assembly was determined to achieve a cessation of hostilities first and then to worry about questions of law and justice. This sentiment was manifest in the margin of support given the United States draft resolution, which was passed overwhelmingly late that evening. Yet the terms of the resolution did go a little beyond ceasefire and withdrawal in their references to the armistice and the Canal.[35]

Immediately after the vote, Lester Pearson, Canadian Minister for External Affairs, rose to explain his delegation's abstention. His first point was also voiced by others. 'Surely we should have used this opportunity to link a cease-fire to the absolute necessity of a political settlement in Palestine and for the Suez [dispute] ... We need action, not only to end the fighting but to make the peace.' To return to the *status quo* would not produce security or peace. It would 'be a return to terror, bloodshed, strife, incidents, charges and countercharges, and ultimately another explosion ...' He concluded with a proposal that the Secretary-General should be authorized to 'begin to make arrangements with Member States for a United Nations force large enough to keep these borders at peace while a political settlement is being worked out'.[36]

Pearson's suggestion was the genesis of the United Nations Emergency Force (U.N.E.F.). Earlier he had transmitted the idea via the Canadian High Commissioner in London to the British Foreign Office. Under pressure in the House of Commons that day, Eden had conceded that Britain would consider such a force to separate Egyptian and Israeli forces. The suggestion had been repeated in the U.N. debate by Sir Pierson Dixon. 'If the United Nations were willing to take over the physical task of maintaining peace in the area', he said, 'no one would be better pleased than

35 Ibid., p. 12 (source of quotation). U.N. GAOR, First Emergency Special Session, 561st Meeting, 1 Nov. 1956, Doc. A/3256, para. 153, pp. 11–12; and 562nd Meeting, 1 Nov. 1956, para. 286, pp. 34–5. The Draft Resolution became General Assembly Resolution (ES–1), 2 Nov. 1956.
36 U.N. GAOR, First Emergency Special Session, 562nd Meeting, 1 Nov. 1956, paras. 304–7, pp. 35–6.

we. But police action there must be, to separate the belligerents and to stop the hostilities.' This British willingness to consider the proposal gave Pearson the impetus to develop the idea further, and to try to convince Hammarskjold and his brains' trust of the feasibility of a United Nations force.[37]

Initial overtures to the Secretary-General were discouraging, however. Hammarskjold doubted that the proposal was practicable or the situation propitious for attempting it. The speeches in the Assembly had been vehement, and Hammarskjold questioned whether the majority of angry Afro-Asian and communist states could be diverted from their violent denunciation of Israel, Britain, and France as aggressors and from their attempt to apply sanctions and coerce withdrawal of the invading forces. As for the United States, the Pearson proposal was rapidly approved by Dulles with Eisenhower's complete agreement. The U.S. was not seeking merely 'to turn the clock back' and would, indeed, welcome from the Canadian delegation 'a concrete suggestion along the lines Mr. Pearson outlined', which appeared to offer Britain and France a face-saving retreat from a position leading to a widening domestic split and vehement international censure.[38]

Finally Pearson, supported by Lodge, was able to persuade Hammarskjold and his special assistant, Andrew Cordier, of the workability of his peace force plan; and by the time the Assembly reconvened in the evening of 3 November, Pearson had the crucial support of Norway, India, and Colombia. This force would not be the British–French force operating under the U.N. flag; that suggestion by Eden had been sharply rebuffed by the Canadian Prime Minister, St. Laurent.

Even so, Eden tried to keep a grip on the Canal by insisting that, before British agreement to a ceasefire, the following conditions should be met: Egypt and Israel would agree to accept a United Nations force stationed between their armies; the force would be maintained until political solutions had been reached for the Suez Canal and Arab–Israeli problems; and Anglo-French troops would separate the combatants until a U.N. force was constituted. These conditions were entirely unacceptable to most members, but they suggested to Pearson that a U.N. force might both satisfy the

[37] Eden, p. 599; U.N. GAOR, First Emergency Special Session, 561st Meeting, 1 Nov. 1956, para. 111, p. 8.

[38] U.N. GAOR, First Emergency Special Session, 562nd Meeting, 1 Nov. 1956, para. 357, p. 39.

vast majority in the Assembly and give Britain and France a face-saving way of extricating themselves.

The Canadian draft resolution, which called upon the Secretary-General to submit a plan within forty-eight hours for the establishment—'with the consent of the nations concerned'—of an international emergency force 'to secure and supervise the cessation of hostilities in accordance with *all* the terms' of Resolution 997 (ES–1), was adopted by a vote of 57 to 0, with 19 abstentions, including the parties to the dispute and the members of the communist bloc. To win the votes of the Arab–Asian bloc, Pearson agreed to support an Arab–Asian resolution demanding a cease-fire within twelve hours, despite its strong condemnatory language.[39]

Although France and in particular Britain had assumed that their forces, then *en route* from Cyprus to Egypt, would be placed under the United Nations flag and become advance units of Pearson's police force, the Arab–Asians and Hammarskjold flatly refused this arrangement. Anglo-French landings, when they occurred, would be in flagrant disregard of the second ceasefire plea, without a shred of the legitimacy which Eden and Pineau had sought to give them. The Pearson police force proposal was not designed as the vehicle for making Britain and France the agents of the United Nations. Its intent was precisely the opposite: to provide them with a face-saving basis for the withdrawal of their forces.

Before any British and French paratroops were dropped along the Canal, the Assembly had approved Resolution 1000, establishing U.N.E.F. and its executive framework and affirming Hammarskjold's decision not to include in it any contingents from permanent members of the Security Council. Consequently, news of the first paratroop landings at 1.00 a.m. 5 November (New York time) fell like a bombshell in New York.[40] The British and French may have hoped to use the leverage of their forces in the Canal Zone to wring concessions on the administration of the Canal from Nasser. But that ambiguous phrase in Resolution 998, 'with the

[39] Ibid., 563rd Meeting, 3 Nov. 1956, para. 285, p. 71. The Canadian draft resolution became Resolution 998 (ES–1) and the Nineteen-Power Proposal was adopted 59 to 5, with 12 abstentions, as Resolution 999 (ES–1).

[40] U.N. GAOR, First Emergency Special Session, Supplement No 1 (A/3354), p. 2. That same afternoon, Bulganin sent the threatening messages mentioned above on p. 63.

consent of the nations concerned', did not mean that Britain and France were being invited to dictate conditions of a political settlement as a prerequisite to replacement of their forces by U.N.E.F. units.

Two United States draft resolutions addressed to the problems of administration of the Suez Canal (A/3273) and of a long-term political settlement between Israel and her Arab neighbours (A/3272) were before the Assembly. The invasion, which the French still hoped would lead to Nasser's removal from power, only intensified the problems of the peacemakers in New York, already complicated by embarrassing Soviet and Chinese offers of volunteers to help Nasser oust the Anglo-French invaders. The Soviet threat underscored the urgency of defining U.N.E.F.'s mandate and moving the force to the Suez Canal. During the early morning hours of 6 November, Hammarskjold cabled the substance of his final report on the formation and composition of an international police force to London and Paris. He and Pearson, assisted by Cordier and Ralph Bunche, had worked feverishly to define the mandate and functions of the force before the main seaborne invasion force arrived from Cyprus. They were too late. Port Said was already under naval bombardment.

The terms of reference for U.N.E.F. were set forth in the Secretary-General's Second and Final Report to the General Assembly pursuant to Resolution 998. Key provisions were that the force was by no means an enforcement body; that it could be stationed only with the consent of the host country; and that it was to be politically neutral and not a diplomatic instrument enabling the invading powers to enhance their bargaining positions. The report emphatically stated 'that there is no intent in the establishment of the Force to influence the military balance in the present conflict and, thereby, the political balance affecting efforts to settle the conflict'.

While the tasks of U.N.E.F. were left open-ended, they were definitely wider than merely 'to secure and supervise the cessation of hostilities' in a strict sense, and included *all* the terms of Resolution 997 of 2 November. Building on this, the Secretary-General stressed that U.N.E.F.'s functions were 'to help maintain quiet during and after' the force withdrawals, and 'to secure compliance with the other terms' of the Resolution. Since the other terms included cessation of raids and 'scrupulously' observing the Armistice Agreements, they potentially opened a significant field of action. The area of U.N.E.F. operations was assumed to cover the whole of Sinai and Gaza, from the Canal to the Egyptian–Israeli borders. Vaguely, the report referred to a 'later stage' when the functions 'should be viewed in the light of efforts over a longer range'; but it did not elaborate.[41]

Pressure on London to abandon the Suez adventure increased during and after 6 November. It was impossible for Eden to maintain credibly that an Anglo-French force in the Canal Zone was necessary to prevent the continuance of hostilities between Israel and Egypt when both states had already accepted a ceasefire. Hammarskjold's cable was evidence of the rapid progress made in New York in the formation of U.N.E.F. Commonwealth support of Britain was almost non-existent. And in Parliament and outside, the Opposition continued to attack the government fiercely, as it had from the start of the intervention. Gaitskell and his associates criticized it on the same grounds which had led Eisenhower to oppose it. They denounced the government for violating the U.N. Charter, jeopardizing the American alliance and the Commonwealth, colluding with Israel, and deceiving Parliament. The press was about equally split pro and con. Like the Parliament and the press, public opinion was deeply divided, largely on party lines; a plurality opposed the intervention initially but gradually shifted to support it. (In mid-October, the Conservative Party Conference had overwhelmingly endorsed the Suez Group's demand for strong action.)[42]

A crucial factor in the weakening British resolve was the attitude of the United States. British oil reserves were rapidly being depleted, yet no move was made to implement contingency plans for diversion of American petroleum to Europe to replace inaccessible Middle East oil. The financial crisis was even more crucial: a run on sterling had developed in New York and other financial markets. On 5 November, the Bank of England alone had spent $300 million to maintain the exchange rate. Attempts to draw on International Monetary Fund reserves were being obstructed by the United States, which refused to consider financial assistance to rescue the pound unless Britain acceded to United Nations recom-

41 Ibid., First Emergency Special Session, Annexes, Doc. A/3302, esp. paras. 7–12, pp. 19–23; approved by Res. 1001, 7 Nov. 1956, ibid., Supplement No. 1 (A/3354).

42 Leon D. Epstein, *British Politics in the Suez Crisis* (University of Illinois Press, Urbana, 1964), esp. chaps. 4, 5, and 7.

mendations and abandoned the Suez invasion. A loan of $1,000 million was promised as soon as Eden decided to withdraw his troops from Suez.[43]

Washington was keeping as distant as possible from its errant allies. British and French queries for American reassurance against Soviet threats elicited a coldly correct reply. 'The Government of the United States', the response read, 'will respect its obligations under the North Atlantic Treaty arrangements.' But Bulganin's proposal that the U.S. and U.S.S.R. join in stopping hostilities was indignantly dismissed by Eisenhower as 'unthinkable', contrary to the U.N. Charter, and an effort to divert world attention from Hungary, where Soviet forces were 'brutally repressing the human rights of the Hungarian people'.[44]

Totally beaten, Eden capitulated at noon on 6 November. As Robertson records the call to Mollet, Eden said: 'I cannot wait. I am under pressure here to bring hostilities to an end today. The best I can do is to postpone it until tonight. We must stop at midnight.' Although Pineau counselled Mollet to let French forces press on alone, the French Cabinet concurred in the British decision. Without a single French officer in a key command position, the French could not carry on alone. In similarly worded letters, Britain and France informed the Secretary-General that their forces would be ordered 'to cease fire at midnight GMT unless attacked', as soon as the Secretary-General could verify that Egypt and Israel had accepted an unconditional ceasefire and that the International force would be competent to implement the operative paragraphs of Assembly Resolution 997 (ES-1). On the night of 6 November, the Anglo-French Suez Expeditionary Force halted about twenty miles south of Port Said.[45]

The next afternoon, the Assembly quickly approved the Secretary-General's guidelines for the organization and functioning of U.N.E.F., authorized Hammarskjold to proceed with the recruitment of contingents, which he had already begun, and established an advisory committee to assist him in implementing plans for the force. Almost immediately, Hammarskjold announced Egyptian consent, in principle, to the entry of General E. L. M.

[43] Robertson, pp. 258–64; Sherman Adams, *Firsthand Report*, pp. 260–70.
[44] Robertson, p. 253.
[45] Ibid., p. 264 (1st quotation); U.N. GAOR, First Emergency Special Session, Annexes, Doc. A/3306 and A/3307, 6 Nov. 1956, pp. 27–8 (2nd quotation).

Burns, Commander of U.N.E.F., and a contingent of ten U.N.E.F. observers. His notification to the governments of the United Kingdom and France that he was fully convinced that U.N.E.F. would be capable of implementing its mandate under Resolution 997 (ES–1) signalled the close of the first phase of United Nations involvement in the Suez Crisis, which the Israeli, British, and French assault on Egypt had initiated.[46]

The ten-day span from 29 October to 7 November was unique in international peacekeeping operations. Much of the credit must go to Lester Pearson. During most of the initial phase, he was the channel for communication between London and Washington. The moral, political, and economic pressure from Washington was crucial, yet Pearson's rescue manoeuvres were equally significant. When the mood of the Assembly was one of condemnation, Pearson offered a constructive alternative that turned the indignation of Arabs and Asians towards support of a novel scheme of direct United Nations peacekeeping which side-stepped, at least initially, the question of blame and guilt. The consensus was achieved in part by ambiguities in the Canadian draft resolutions, which would plague Hammarskjold as he tried to implement them.

Together with Hammarskjold and his aides, Pearson tailored the force to the specifications of the Suez Crisis. To Hammarskjold, executive of U.N.E.F. and co-author of the guidelines under which it operated, was entrusted the responsibility for putting the force into the field once a ceasefire had been achieved and Britain and France had agreed in principle to the removal of their troops.

[46] Ibid., First Emergency Special Session, Annexes, Res. 1001 (ES–1), 7 Nov. 1956, p. 34; U.N., Department of Public Information, Press Services, Press Release SG/518, 7 Nov. 1956; U.N. GAOR, First Emergency Special Session, Annexes, Doc. A/3314, 7 Nov. 1956, p. 31.

V

RETURN TO THE *STATUS QUO*?

AFTER the ceasefire, the withdrawal of forces became the critical issue. When an attack has been provoked by violations of international obligations, must the attacker withdraw before his grievances are considered? Or should some protection against future violations be concurrent with withdrawal? U.N.E.F. offered one means for providing such protection, if it could be worked out. Yet the efforts to put U.N.E.F. into the field and to establish its status brought out sharply its tenuous legal foundations and its fragility.

In the struggle over these issues, legal norms were invoked for pressure or defence by all major parties, especially the U.S., Israel, Egypt, and the U.N.

1. ENTRY AND OPERATION OF U.N.E.F.

The phrase 'with the consent of the nations concerned', which had had useful ambiguity on 3 November, returned to haunt Hammarskjold as soon as he tried to implement his mandate and arrange for U.N.E.F.'s entry into Egypt. Nasser, intensely jealous of Egypt's sovereignty, was fearful that U.N.E.F. might become an instrument of Anglo-French pressure to internationalize the Suez Canal. His suspicions were not unfounded, for during the debate on Resolution 1001 (ES–1), Sir Pierson Dixon had indicated his government's position that British and French troops were unlikely to withdraw before U.N.E.F. could replace them. It was Eden's hope that British forces could be used to 'shape a lasting settlement for the Arab–Israeli conflict and for the future of the Canal.'[1]

Nasser, in seeking to prevent U.N.E.F. from becoming a political instrument of the occupiers, had two allies with great powers of persuasion and authority, the United States and the Secretary-General. Eden was subjected to steady pressure from Washington

[1] U.N. GAOR, 567th Meeting, 7 Nov. 1956, paras. 100, 102, pp. 112–13; Eden, p. 625 (quotation).

to withdraw Anglo-French forces.[1a] Eisenhower, whose concern was
to get the British out, did not share Eden's assessment of the situation in the area, and he was not prepared to discuss and concert
policy with Britain before Anglo-French forces were withdrawn
from Egypt. In no way would the United States permit Britain to
gain an advantage from action which it regarded as a flagrant
violation of the U.N. Charter.[2] Hammarskjold, on his part, had
clearly established the principle that U.N.E.F. was not designed to
influence either the military or political balance in the conflict.
This was tantamount to saying that the U.N. responsibility was to
restore the *status quo ante*, which had been destroyed by the
resort to force. Yet U.N.E.F.'s impact could not remain neutral
while it was carrying out its mandate of achieving and supervising
the withdrawal of foreign troops from Egyptian territory; in giving
withdrawal precedence over attempts to settle underlying political
problems, Hammarskjold was actually reinforcing the Egyptian
position whatever his intentions.

The necessity for Egypt's consent to the entry of U.N.E.F. gave
Nasser a tempting lever for control of U.N.E.F. According to
General Burns:

> The Egyptians tried to make it mean that they had a right to say
> what nations should send contingents, where units of the Force should
> be stationed, that their consent would be required whenever a unit was
> moved, and several other conditions which would have been hampering
> in the extreme, if they would not indeed, have made the Force an
> agency of the Egyptian Government, not of the United Nations.[3]

Despite the need for Egypt's consent, the Secretary-General was
not prepared to concede to Nasser complete control over the
stationing and movement of these units, but was determined to
retain decision-making autonomy for U.N.E.F. Therefore his response to initial inquiries from Nasser and Fawzi regarding the
extent of Egyptian control over troop contingents in U.N.E.F. was
not especially reassuring to the Egyptians. The Secretary-General
was unyielding on Canadian participation in the Force, although

[1a] American pressure on the Israeli government was equally unremitting,
but since the problems were of a different nature, this aspect of the Suez
Crisis will be treated separately.

[2] Eden, pp. 629–31, and Eisenhower, pp. 93–4; Sherman Adams, *Firsthand
Report*, pp. 260–70.

[3] Lt.-Gen. E. L. M. Burns, *Between Arab and Israeli* (George C. Harrap and
Co., Ltd., London, 1962), p. 193.

he was willing to defer to Egyptian wishes not to include a Canadian infantry unit. Eventually, Egypt agreed to accept Canadian logistical and medical support units.

The entry of Burns and the ten U.N.E.F. observers was held up for four days while Nasser and the Secretary-General exchanged views on the duration of U.N.E.F.'s stay. Nasser maintained that since Egyptian consent was necessary for U.N.E.F.'s entry, withdrawal of consent would require the withdrawal of U.N.E.F. from Egypt. Although the view was consistent with his own admission of Egypt's sovereign rights, the Secretary-General rejected it, insisting that the U.N. forces were entitled to remain until the completion of their prescribed task. He wrote to Nasser that as long as that task was not completed 'the reasons for the consent of the government remained valid, hence withdrawal of consent prior to completion of the task would run counter to the acceptance by Egypt of the decision of the General Assembly. If a difference were to develop, whether or not the reasons for the arrangements were still valid, the matter would be brought up for negotiation with the United Nations.'[4] When he threatened to refer the issue to the Assembly, Egypt permitted Burns to come to Cairo, implicitly acquiescing in Hammarskjold's view of the matter.

The *aide-mémoire* which summarized areas of agreement between President Nasser and the Secretary-General, hammered out on 17 November in Cairo, was less specific than the Hammarskjold letter, although it, too, embodied the Secretary-General's view, in language acceptable to the government of Egypt. At first Nasser was extremely reluctant to accept the far-reaching restrictions on Egyptian sovereignty implied by the Assembly's broad definition of U.N.E.F.'s tasks, but he was finally persuaded to acquiesce in the 'good faith' formula Hammarskjold had proposed. The General Assembly approved the *aide mèmoire* on 26 November.[5]

The 'good faith' agreement in the *aide mémoire* sought to balance two principles: (1) the right of the Assembly to determine the tasks of the Emergency Force and the basis on which it was to fulfil its mission, and (2) the necessity for consent of the govern-

---

[4] Ernest A. Gross, *The United Nations: Structure for Peace* (Harper & Row, New York, 1962), p. 31. This account is based on Hammarskjold's so-called secret memorandum, reprinted in *N.Y. Times*, 19 June, 1967.

[5] U.N. GAOR, 11th Session, 1956-7, Plenary Meetings 1, 26 Nov. 1956, Plenary Meeting 596th, p. 343.

ment on whose territory the force would operate. In practice it reflected the precarious relation among the interests of Egypt, of the United Nations, of the governments sending troops, and of other governments. In the final formula, Egypt agreed that 'when exercising its sovereign rights on any matter concerning the presence and functioning of UNEF, it will be guided, in good faith, by its acceptance of General Assembly Resolution 1000 (ES–1) of 5 November 1956.' And the Secretary-General, for the U.N. undertook that 'the activities of UNEF will be guided, in good faith, by the task established for the Force,' and that U.N.E.F. would be maintained until its task was completed. Two other memos, not published, covered the U.N.E.F. entry into Egypt and the reopening of the Canal.[6]

Hammarskjold elaborated on the *aide-mémoire* in the so-called secret memo of 5 August, 1957, published after withdrawal of U.N.E.F. from Sinai in May 1967, at the request of the government of Egypt. In that document, the Secretary-General explained that rather than limit Egyptian sovereignty 'by a basic understanding requesting an agreement *directly concerning* withdrawal, we created an obligation to reach agreement on the fact that the tasks were completed, and, thus, the conditions for a withdrawal established'.[7]

Nasser was extremely sensitive about the U.N.E.F. presence in the area of the Suez Canal, insisting that U.N.E.F. should operate there only as long as non-Egyptian forces remained in that region. The Secretary-General concurred in the Egyptian view and assured Nasser that 'except for a possible staging area in the region of the Canal, UNEF would have no functions there once that area ceased to be a battle zone.' At the first meeting of the advisory committee on 14 November, Hammarskjold stated that U.N.E.F. 'shall have no function in the Canal Zone after the Anglo-French withdrawal, and that the force will in no way take over from the Anglo-French forces'.[8]

Although Nasser was very eager to have the Canal reopened, he remained adamant that British and French salvage units must

---

[6] Ibid.; Brian Urquhart, *Hammarskjold: The Years of Decision*, pp. 191–2.

[7] *N.Y. Times*, 19 June 1967 (emphasis in the original). See Urquhart, pp. 193–4.

[8] William R. Frye, *A United Nations Peace Force* (Oceana Publications, Inc., New York, 1957), p. 14; Terence Robertson, *Crisis: The Inside Story of the Suez Conspiracy*, p. 289.

be excluded from the clearing operation. The Secretary-General's own reticence about admitting British or French salvage crews hardened rapidly into total rejection of their use. British offers of assistance also received a sharp rebuff in New York and Washington. And Nasser demanded that British and French troops withdraw completely before he would permit salvage operations to begin.

Yet, every day the Canal remained blocked, the oil situation in Western Europe became more precarious. There was no indication when or whether the United States intended to implement its emergency plans for increasing the quota of Western hemisphere oil available to Europeans. In Washington, it was hoped that this continued uncertainty might hasten a British and French decision to evacuate their forces from Egypt. The U.S. was unwilling to risk what influence it still had with the Arabs by appearing to co-operate with Britain and France so long as these states refused to implement Assembly withdrawal requests. Thus the British and French were caught between conflicting desires and necessities.

The British government was determined, however, to see definite arrangements made for clearing the Canal before ordering more than a token withdrawal of allied forces. Furthermore, the British intended to make complete troop withdrawal conditional on the resumption of negotiations about the future administration of the Canal. Yet token withdrawal did not satisfy Washington's demands for substantial compliance with Assembly resolutions, the precondition for American support in alleviating the oil shortage and further bolstering the shaky position of the pound sterling. An O.E.E.C. report had gloomily stated that failure to implement the emergency oil supply plan might have long-term adverse effects on the European balance of payments situation, resulting in austerity programmes and an absolute reduction in living standards. Still, Washington remained firm. A British statement on 22 November that withdrawal 'was about to begin' was judged an insufficient guarantee of the British commitment to withdraw all forces from Suez promptly. Even intense American pressure could not spur the British government to an unequivocal undertaking to withdraw from Egypt promptly without independent assurances that U.N.E.F. would be more than simply an Egyptian vehicle for getting rid of foreign troops.[9]

[9] The policy discussions in the U.S. regarding oil supply are described in detail in Sherman Adams, *Firsthand Report*, pp. 260-70.

Assembly debate on Suez, from 23 to 27 November, was hardly reassuring to the Eden government. Krishna Menon of India led the impatient Arab–Asian group in demanding harsh condemnation of Britain, France, and Israel for failure to comply with previous resolutions. Finally, pressure from Washington and the likelihood of castigation by the General Assembly forced a definite British commitment to withdraw. On 21 November, Selwyn Lloyd, British Foreign Secretary, informed the Secretary-General that the Anglo-French forces would be withdrawn

as soon as Her Majesty's Government are satisfied that UNEF is in a position to assume effectively the tasks assigned to it under the Assembly resolutions.... [That was not yet the case since] the UNEF is still in a process of being built up....

Nevertheless the United Kingdom Government, as an indication of their intentions, have decided to withdraw at once an infantry battalion from Port Said. The withdrawal of other units will proceed as the United Nations Force becomes effective.[10]

In similar communications, France informed the Secretary-General that one-third of its forces had already departed, and Israel stated that two battalions had been withdrawn from Egyptian territory. These indications of compliance succeeded only in obtaining a slight moderation of the wording of the resolution. As amended, it expressed regret that large contingents of foreign troops were still in Egypt and reiterated the earlier appeal for immediate and complete British, French, and Israeli compliance with Assembly resolutions calling for withdrawal of all non-Egyptian forces.[11]

The harsh Afro-Asian resolution, to which the United States gave its support, rapidly led to an impasse: Britain and France would not move to comply with the highly critical resolution nor could they ignore it. The United States had fallen in step with the United Nations, and in that forum action was being held up by Nasser's suspicious nature. Accordingly, an elaborate scheme with interlocking, interdependent elements was concocted by Pearson and Hammarskjold to break the deadlock. The scenario consisted of a series of conditional commitments, each of which was vital

[10] U.N. GAOR, 11th Session, Annexes, Doc. A/3384, Annex 3, 21 Nov. 1956, paras. 3–4, p. 17.

[11] Ibid., Doc. A/3384, Annex 1, 21 Nov. 1956, and Annex 8, 24 Nov. 1956, paras. 3–4, p. 17; ibid., Res. 1120 (XI), 24 Nov. 1956, p. 75.

to the total operation: Hammarskjold would announce the actual strength of U.N.E.F., and Lloyd would accept this indication of its competence as the basis for announcing total British troop withdrawal by 14 December. At the same time, he would suggest a resumption of the private talks on the administration of the Suez Canal, on the basis of the 'Six Principles' for a Canal settlement agreed upon in October by the U.N. Nasser, according to plan, was then to announce co-operation on beginning clearance operations, and Hammarskjold was to report that U.N. salvage crews would start to clear the Canal on 15 December.

The stages proceeded almost on schedule and as planned. After receiving notes from France and the United Kingdom on 3 December, informing him of their decisions to withdraw completely, Hammarskjold promptly instructed General Burns to arrange with the commander of the Anglo-French forces for U.N.E.F. units to take over the responsibility for maintaining quiet in the areas begin evacuated by British and French units. British and French withdrawal was complete, not by 14 December as hoped, but by 22 December.[12]

The scenario for Canal clearance was not respected by the principal parties. The British and French *notes verbales* referred to the Six Principles for Canal administration, as previously arranged, but Nasser refused to commit himself to them as the basis for resuming three-power discussions under the Secretary-General's auspices. Thereafter, the British government partially repudiated Lloyd's offer of 23 November of full British support for U.N. salvage operations, including 'willingness to release salvage ships under charter to the British Admiralty or to the United Kingdom Government'. On the basis of this offer, Hammarskjold had obtained from Fawzi permission 'to use any equipment he considered necessary', provided non-Egyptian forces withdrew. No agreement had been reached on the question of crews. On 7 December, Sir Pierson Dixon informed the Secretary-General that 'the Anglo-French salvage fleet, with its administrative support, is a single unit which must either stay as a whole or go as a whole'. Confirming this position, R. A. Butler, as acting Prime Minister in Eden's absence, on 13 December announced that British salvage ships would serve only with British crews, effectively removing the six heavy-lift ships in the Anglo-French fleet from the U.N. salvage

---

[12] Ibid., Doc. A/3415, 3 Dec. 1956, pp. 28–9.

force. In the United Nations, this action was seen as an attempt to obstruct the clearance operation.[13]

As soon as the Anglo-French military forces had left Port Said, the United Nations assumed responsibility for the salvage operations which the British had begun. Aside from their clearance operations in Port Said harbour, the British and French were totally excluded from any role in re-opening the Suez Canal. Along the length of the Canal, only ships and salvage crews under contract to the United Nations were employed. The last obstruction to Canal transit was raised on 8 April, 1957—more than a month ahead of schedule.

2. GETTING THE ISRAELIS OUT

Inducing Israel to relinquish the territory gained in the attack presented a separate problem which took four months of bargaining and pressure to resolve. For eight years Israel had borne the burden of what its leaders viewed as a one-sided application of the Charter. Time and again Soviet vetoes had blocked attempts to reprimand Egypt for raids across the armistice demarcation line in violation of the armistice agreements. No one had exercised the veto for Israel's benefit, and Israeli military retaliation had repeatedly been noted and condemned by the Security Council. The armistice agreements had been too feeble to halt Arab raids and the application of sanctions too one-sided to inspire Israeli faith in the agreements or in the United Nations as a neutral arbiter of Arab–Israeli quarrels. By the time of the joint attack on Egypt, Israel was convinced that its claims were solidly based in law and justice.

When Israeli forces ceased fighting on 4 November, they held much of the Sinai Peninsula, the Gaza Strip, and the land and island points controlling the Gulf of Aqaba. The last two areas were strategic gains: administrative control of Gaza gave Israel control over the bases for the fedayeen raids; and possession of Sharm el-Sheikh and the Straits of Tiran enabled Israel to take advantage of the shorter shipping route to Asia and Africa via the Persian Gulf to Eilat, thus by-passing the Suez Canal, which had been closed by Egypt to Israeli or Israel-bound shipping. These were benefits which Ben-Gurion wanted to retain, if possible.

[13] Ibid., 591st Meeting, 23 Nov. 1956, para. 98, p. 259; Urquhart, pp. 198–201 (quotation on p. 199).

His first approach was a strong one. On 7 November, he announced to the Knesset that 'the armistice agreement with Egypt was dead and could not be restored'—presumably opening the possibility of keeping control of these strategic areas. This position at once provoked a severe official U.S. reaction and a letter from Eisenhower warning that it endangered the peace efforts, risked grave consequences for Israel, and 'might impair the friendly cooperation between our two countries'. Bulganin sent a note menacing in tone and content.[14]

Ben-Gurion took a step back. His 8 November reply to Eisenhower stated:

Neither I nor any other authorized spokesman of the government of Israel has stated that we plan to annex the Sinai desert [no mention of Gaza]. In view of the U.N. resolutions regarding the withdrawal of foreign troops from Egypt and the creation of an international force we will upon the conclusion of satisfactory arrangements with the U.N. in connection with this international force entering the Suez Canal area, willingly withdraw our forces.[15]

An *aide-mémoire* of 21 November set out the Israeli position on withdrawal from these areas:

1. There has been a withdrawal of Israel's forces for varying distances along the entire Egyptian front.
2. [As stated on 8 November 1956] ... Israel will willingly withdraw its forces from Egypt immediately upon the conclusion of satisfactory arrangements with the United Nations in connection with the Emergency International Force. The "satisfactory arrangements," which Israel seeks are such as will ensure Israel security against the recurrence of the threat or danger of attack, and against acts of belligerency by land or sea.

. . . . .

4. The Government of Israel ... waits information on the proposed size, location, and stationing arrangements of the United Nations Emergency Force, and on the method proposed for the discharge of all the functions laid down in the resolutions of 2, 5, and 7 November ... [which] include various provisions, in addition to those for the cease-fire and withdrawal of forces.[16]

[14] Urquhart, p. 182 (1st quotation); David Ben-Gurion, *Israel: A Personal History*, pp. 508–12 (2nd quotation on p. 510).
[15] Department of State, *Middle East*, p. 213.
[16] U.N. GAOR, 11th Session, Annexes, Doc. A/3384, Annex 2, 21 Nov. 1956, pp. 16–17.

At the year's end (29 December) Mrs. Meir met with Dulles and presented the heart of Israel's position: 'We were therefore asking him to announce support for freedom of passage in the Straits of Eilat and the nonreturn to Egypt of the Gaza Strip; to persuade Hammarskjold to postpone any changes in Sinai and the Gaza Strip until a settlement was reached and agreed to; and to obtain a United States guarantee of freedom of navigation in the Straits.'[17] But matters quickly reached an impasse. Israel refused to withdraw unless U.N.E.F. could guarantee freedom of navigation and an end to fedayeen raids, while Hammarskjold insisted that Israel return to the positions its forces had held when the fighting broke out and that it not prescribe any conditions for withdrawal. As a result, when retreating Israeli forces reached the eastern edge of Sinai on 22 January, they halted. Ben-Gurion made it clear that further withdrawals from the Sharm el-Sheikh area and the Gaza Strip would not be undertaken unilaterally, or without guarantees for Israel's security.

In effect, Israel was demanding, as it had suggested before, that the fundamental security problems be tackled at the same time that a full and complete withdrawal was being negotiated. Abba Eban had stated his government's position in the first hours of Assembly consideration of the crisis: 'It will not do to go back to an outdated and crumbling armistice regime designed by its authors to last for a few months and now lingering for eight years in growing paralysis of function.'[18] Thus the U.N. approach to the crisis was the position least acceptable to Israel—full return to the armistice lines as a precondition for beginning to resolve the basic political problems between Egypt and Israel.

Hammarskjold, empowered to implement Assembly recommendations, adopted an ever more rigid stance as Israeli intractability persisted. On 15 January 1957, he stressed that the basic Assembly resolution imposed no conditional linkage among the injunctions 'to withdraw all forces behind the armistice lines, to desist from raids across the armistice lines ... and to observe scrupulously the provisions of the armistice agreement'. In Hammarskjold's view, the provisions of that resolution were to be satisfied sequentially: ceasefire, withdrawal, and only then attention to the long-range problems of a settlement. The

[17] Ben-Gurion, p. 523.
[18] U.N. GAOR, First Emergency Special Session, Annexes, Resolution, 562nd Meeting, 1 Nov. 1956, para. 158, p. 24.

Secretary-General elaborated on his view in his report to the Assembly:

Like the cease-fire, withdrawal is a preliminary and essential phase in a development through which a stable basis may be laid for peaceful conditions in the area.... [The] high priority [given by the General Assembly resolutions] to the cease-fire and the withdrawal ... reflected both basic principles of the Charter and essential political considerations.

The Assembly, in taking this position, in no way disregarded all the other aims which must be achieved in order to create more satisfactory conditions than those prevailing during the period preceding the crisis. Some of these aims were mentioned by the Assembly. Others are to be found in previous decisions of the United Nations. All of them call for urgent attention. The basic function of the United Nations Emergency Force, 'to help maintain quiet,' gives the Force great value as a background for efforts toward resolving such pending problems, *although it is not itself a means to that end.*

It is essential that, through prompt conclusion of the first phases of implementation of the General Assembly resolutions, Member Governments should now be enabled to turn to the constructive tasks to which the establishment and maintenance of the cease-fire, a full withdrawal of forces behind the armistice lines, a desisting from raids and scrupulous observance of the armistice agreements, should open the way.[19]

Hammarskjold made clear that he was not trying to shelve the long-term problems, which had to be settled to restore genuine peace in the Middle East. He was, however, fundamentally opposed to negotiation under the pressure of Israeli occupation of strategic bridgeheads in Egyptian territory. His position reflected the determination of the Assembly that Israel should receive no advantage from illegal actions: the gains won by Israeli resort to force could not be permitted to become the basis for permanent settlement terms or used for leverage in the negotiations.

On 24 January Hammarskjold again argued that full and complete Israeli withdrawal behind the armistice lines was of first importance. He knew that the armistice agreements were disputed and that the rights they conferred had not been observed; yet he insisted that they furnished the only legal basis for moving to negotiations. 'Whatever the state of non-compliance with the Armistice Agreements in general before the crisis', by-passing them

[19] Ibid., 11th Session, Annexes, Doc. A/3500, 15 Jan. 1957, paras. 15–17, p. 44.

would seriously impede progress towards solving problems, whereas carrying out Articles 7 and 8 fully would contribute to relaxing tensions and creating peaceful conditions in the region.

Hammarskjold based his position on three principles:

(a) The United Nations cannot condone a change of the *status juris* resulting from military action contrary to the provisions of the Charter. ... [It must, therefore, restore the prior *status juris* by requiring withdrawal of forces and foregoing any territorial claims based on the military action.]

(b) The use of military force by the United Nations other than that under Chapter VII of the Charter [1] requires the consent of the States in which the Force is to operate.... [2] must be undertaken and developed in a manner consistent with the principles mentioned under (a) above.... [3] must ... not serve as a means to force settlement, in the interest of one party, of political conflicts or legal issues recognized as controversial.

(c) United Nations actions must respect fully the rights of Member Governments recognized in the Charter, and international agreements not contrary to the aims of the Charter, which are concluded in exercise of those rights.[20]

Hammarskjold's view was challenged by Abba Eban:

Our view is simple.... In the three outstanding issues—the Suez Canal, the Gulf of Aqaba, and the Gaza Strip—our duty is not to re-establish but to prevent the re-establishment of the previous situation, for in each case the situation of 28 October 1956 was one of illegalities and not of law.... These three illegalities, more than any other factors, brought about the hostilities which we are now seeking to liquidate. In pursuing its policy for the withdrawal of non-Egyptian troops the United Nations surely has no duty to restore Egypt's blockading and raiding capacity to its former state.[21]

Israel maintained steadfastly that the armistice agreement was indivisible, and that a ceasefire at the demarcation lines was insufficient without absolute observance of *all* the terms—not only an end to border raids and scrupulous observance of the armistice lines but also an end to the blockade of the Gulf of Aqaba and of the Suez Canal to Israeli shipping.

On the blockades, Hammarskjold could give no firm assurance of Egyptian intentions, for it was precisely these responsibilities which Egypt had disputed, arguing that the blockades were legiti-

---

[20] Ibid., Doc. A/3512, 24 Jan. 1957, para. 16, p. 48, and para. 5, p. 47.
[21] Ibid., 11th Session, 645th Meeting, 28 Jan. 1957, para 18, p. 982.

mate acts in exercise of belligerent rights. The Secretary-General could only hope that a return to the ceasefire would lead to respect for all the terms of the armistice agreement:

Were the substantive clauses of the Armistice Agreement, especially Articles VII and VIII, again to be implemented, the case against all acts of belligerency, which is based on the existence of the Armistice regime, would gain full cogency. With such a broader implementation of the Armistice Agreement, the parties should be asked to give assurances that, on the basis established, they will not assert any belligerent rights (including, of course, such rights in the Gulf of Aqaba and the Straits of Tiran).[22]

Hammarskjold based his argument on the 1951 Security Council resolution denying Egyptian claims of belligerent rights, which Egypt had never accepted or implemented. Israel could well be unconvinced by this line of reasoning, for there were no indications that Nasser was any more disposed to honour the Security Council resolution in 1957 than in the period before the Israeli attack.

Every Israeli attempt to assure that, after withdrawal, her borders and rights would be guaranteed by something more substantial than an oft-flouted paper accord was rejected by Hammarskjold. He flatly refused to tolerate any change in the status of the Gaza Strip, either by Israeli civilian control or United Nations administration. Gaza had been under Egyptian control prior to the attack, and without regard for Israeli objections to the *de facto* administrative situation there before 29 October 1956, Hammarskjold insisted that control had to revert to Egypt before Israeli claims could be considered. The implications for U.N.E.F. were clear: 'Deployment of UNEF, in Gaza, under the resolutions of the General Assembly, would have to be on the same basis as its deployment along the armistice line in the Sinai Peninsula. Any broader function for it in that area, in view of the terms of the Armistice Agreement and a recognized principle of international law, would require the consent of Egypt.'[23] Such a position did not leave much latitude for manoeuvring. Israel refused to withdraw from Gaza without at least some measure of U.N.E.F. administration, and Hammarskjold refused to discuss such guarantees until Israeli withdrawal was complete. Even so, the Secretary-

[22] Ibid., 11th Session, Annexes, Doc. A/3512, para. 27, p. 49.
[23] Ibid., paras. 13, 14, p. 48.

General did cautiously suggest the possibility that U.N.E.F. might 'assist in maintaining quiet in the area', beyond its duties during actual Israeli troop withdrawal. While U.N.E.F. was 'not to be deployed in such a way as to protect any special position on these questions', it might transitionally 'function in support of mutual restraint ...'[24]

Although Hammarskjold appeared to be leaving room for negotiations, the majority of the U.N. members were insistent that U.N.E.F. not become an occupation force or a means of supporting one side in any eventual political negotiations. In direct refutation of the United States view that U.N.E.F. could be used to restrain attempts to exercise belligerent rights or hostilities contrary to the armistice agreement, Fawzi argued for Egypt:

The United Nations Emergency Force is in Egypt not as an occupation force, not as a replacement for the invaders, not to resolve any question or to settle any problems, be that problem in relation to the Suez Canal, to Palestine or to freedom of passage in territorial waters. It is not there to infringe upon Egyptian sovereignty in any fashion or to any extent but, on the contrary, for the sole purpose of giving expression to the determination of the United Nations to put an end to the aggression committed against Egypt and securing the withdrawal of Israel behind the armistice demarcation line.[25]

The Assembly did not agree completely with the Egyptian position; yet it was rent by such internal splits that it was unable to reach any consensus on a reaffirmation or broadening of Hammarskjold's mandate. The Secretary-General's hint that U.N.E.F. could function as a buffer, even in undisputed Egyptian territory, was endorsed by the Assembly in its Resolution 1125 (XI). The resolution affirmed the Secretary-General's view that the prerequisite for long-term progress in the Middle East was a return to the armistice agreement, beginning with complete withdrawal of Israeli forces to positions behind the demarcation lines. United Nations forces were given the task of remaining on the armistice lines; in effect, they were charged with supervising compliance with the armistice. The resolution further recognized that a return to the armistice would not signal the end of United Nations responsibilities but the transition to a new phase of the problem, that of 'creation of peaceful conditions' facilitating co-operation towards the attain-

[24] Ibid., para. 29, p. 49.
[25] Ibid., 11th Session, 651st Meeting, 2 Feb. 1957, para. 154, p. 1073.

ment of 'objectives transcending the immediate issues at stake', as Hammarskjold defined it in his 24 January report to the General Assembly.[26]

To be effective, U.N.E.F. had to have the support and confidence of the governments of both Israel and Egypt. It could not be used, as Hammarskjold had emphasized, to force a settlement of political conflicts or controversial legal issues in the interest of one party. It had to represent a neutral, impartial instrument of the world community. But did neutrality require a return to the *status quo ante?*

Hammarskjold seemed to think so. As he had indicated on 15 January, he refused in principle to use U.N.E.F. to try to solve substantive issues without express authority from the General Assembly. Denied this mandate, which Pearson urged the Assembly to grant, Hammarskjold adopted a very pragmatic approach, moving cautiously to obtain Israeli troop withdrawal from Gaza and Sharm el-Sheikh and to restore the situation before hostilities. But his position made it extremely difficult for him to obtain Israeli withdrawal. He was unable to offer Israel assurances with regard to U.N.E.F. control of Gaza; and although he had privately supported the Israeli legal position on the right to free passage through the Gulf of Aqaba, he did not make this view public.[27]

The Ben-Gurion government, frustrated in New York, sought assurances in Washington that complete troop withdrawal would not be the signal for a return to the old tensions—for fedayeen raids out of Gaza, blockade of the Straits of Tiran, denial of the Suez Canal to Israeli or Israel-bound shipping. To buttress the Israeli rights in the Straits of Tiran, Eban gave Dulles a legal *aide-mémoire* stating that the Straits were an international waterway because:

1. They provided access to four littoral states bordering on the Gulf.
2. They constituted the only passage to and from the port of Eilat.
3. The International Court of Justice had ruled that in straits constituting a waterway serving more than one country, all states have the right of navigation, even if the straits fall wholly or partly within the territorial waters of one country or another.

---

[26] Ibid., Annexes, Res. 1125 (XI), 2 Feb. 1957, p. 76; ibid., Doc. A/3512, para. 34, p. 50.
[27] See Hammarskjold's two reports to the General Assembly. U.N. GAOR, 11th Session, Annexes, Doc. A/3500, 15 Jan. 1957, paras. 13–14, pp. 43–4, and Doc. A/3512, 24 Jan. 1957, paras. 24–34, p. 49.

4. The Security Council in 1951 rejected an Egyptian claim of the right to search or seize ships headed for Israel.

5. The United States had declared in the Security Council that the 1951 principle applied also to the Gulf of Aqaba (Eilat).

6. In reply to a question by the U.S. government in January 1950 Egypt had stated that passage through the Straits of Tiran would remain free as it had in the past 'in accordance with international law.'[28]

The stress on international legality seemed to make an impression on Dulles. On 11 February, he transmitted a statement of the U.S. position to Ambassador Eban. The *aide-mémoire* contained two suggestions—that U.N.E.F. be deployed on the border between Israel and the Gaza Strip, and that, as a precautionary measure, U.N.E.F. enter the territory controlling access to the Straits of Tiran as Israeli forces withdrew. The United States declared itself prepared to use its influence in concert with other United Nations members to attain other measures aimed at a long-term settlement following Israeli troop withdrawal. One other commitment was of particular interest to Israel: the United States declared its belief that 'no nation has the right to prevent free and innocent passage in the Gulf [of Aqaba] and through the Straits giving access thereto', as well as its readiness to exercise the right of free and innocent passage in the Straits of Tiran and 'to join with others to secure general recognition of this right'.[29]

But Israel still held back, waiting for concrete guarantees before withdrawal. On 2 February, the Assembly had adopted two resolutions: one calling on Israel to withdraw and the other for measures to create a more stable peace after withdrawal. In his report of 11 February to the Assembly, Hammarskjold left no doubts about the relationship between withdrawal and a long-term settlement:

The relationship between the two resolutions on withdrawal [Assembly Resolution 1124] and on measures to be carried out after withdrawal [Assembly Resolution 1125] affords the possibility of informal explorations of the whole field covered by the resolutions, preparatory to negotiations.... However, such explorations cannot be permitted to invert the sequence between withdrawal and other measures.[30]

[28] Ben-Gurion, pp. 524–5.

[29] Department of State Press Release 72, 17 Feb. 1957, reprinted in *Middle East*, pp. 290–2.

[30] U.N. GAOR, 11th Session, Annexes, Doc. A/3527, 11 Feb. 1957, para. 17, p. 59.

Dissatisfied with both the Assembly resolutions and the American statement of 11 February, the Ben-Gurion government continued to seek guarantees as a precondition for withdrawal.

Eisenhower, warned by Lodge that the Afro-Asian nations, joined by the Arab and Communist states, were likely to propose sanctions within a week, decided to clarify the U.S. position despite strong opposition from Congressional leaders. On the evening of 20 February, he said in a television talk that Israel's insistence on guarantees as a condition for withdrawal raised a basic question of principle:

Should a nation which attacks and occupies foreign territory in the face of United Nations disapproval be allowed to impose conditions on its own withdrawal?

If we agree that armed attack can properly achieve the purposes of the assailant, then I fear we will have turned back the clock of international order. We will, in effect, have countenanced the use of force as a means of settling international differences and through this gaining international advantages.

If the United Nations first admits that international disputes can be settled by using force, then we will have destroyed the very foundation of the organization, and our best hope of establishing a world order. That would be a disaster for us all.

Eisenhower made it clear that the United States would support the United Nations if there were 'no choice but to exert pressure upon Israel to comply with the withdrawal resolutions'. He added, 'Of course, we still hope that the Government of Israel will see that its best immediate and long-term interests lie in compliance with the United Nations and in placing its trust in the resolution of the United Nations and in the declaration of the United States with reference to the future.'[31]

This was sufficient to encourage Israel to consider concrete withdrawal measures. On 22 February the Secretary-General indicated that the takeover of Gaza 'would, in the first instance, be exclusively by U.N.E.F.', a vague statement open to differing interpretations by Egypt and Israel. On the same day Afghanistan, Indonesia, Iran, Lebanon, Pakistan, and the Sudan introduced a daft resolution condemning Israel for its failure to withdraw and calling on all states 'to deny all military, economic or financial assistance and facilities to Israel in view of its continued defiance'

[31] *Dep't of State Bull.*, 11 Mar. 1957, pp. 387–91; Department of State, *Middle East*, pp. 301–7 (quotations on pp. 304, 306–7).

of the withdrawal resolutions.[32] As various Arab diplomats de-nounced Israel, the U.S. withheld comment on the draft resolution, again using the tactic of ominous silence to press for a reversal of Israeli policy.

On 1 March, the government of Israel succumbed. Golda Meir delivered the surrender message: 'The Government of Israel is now in a position to announce its plans for full and prompt with-drawal from the Sharm el-Sheikh area and the Gaza Strip, in compliance with General Assembly resolution 1124 (XI) of 2 February 1957.'[33] The withdrawal was based on certain 'under-standings' regarding the subsequent deployment of U.N.E.F. and the willingness of maritime powers to exercise their right of free and independent passage in the Gulf of Aqaba and the Straits of Tiran.

Mrs. Meir was followed by Lodge:

The United States also takes note of the declarations made in the statement of the representative of Israel. We do not consider that these declarations make Israel's withdrawal 'conditional.' For the most part the declarations constitute, as we understand it, restatements of what has already been said by the Assembly or by the Secretary-General in his reports, or hopes and expectations which seem to us not unreasonable in the light of the prior actions of the Assembly.[34]

His description of the Israeli understandings as 'not unreasonable' rather than as 'justifiable', came as an unpleasant shock to Mrs. Meir. Next day, to make the U.S. attitude clearer, the President wrote to Ben-Gurion that he believed 'Israel would have no cause for regret' and that the Israeli hopes and expectations were 'reason-able'.[35]

On 4 March General Dayan and General Burns reached agree-ment on the technical details of the withdrawal and takeover. During the night of 7–8 March, withdrawing Israeli troops were replaced by U.N.E.F. in the Gaza Strip, and on 8 March the trans-fer of authority—on an emergency basis—was completed there and in Sharm el-Sheikh.

A week later, Nasser sent an Egyptian administrative governor

[32] U.N. GAOR, 11th Session, 659th Meeting, 22 February 1957, para. 26, p. 1192; ibid., Annexes, Doc. A/3557, 22 Feb. 1957, esp. para. 2, p. 62.
[33] Ibid., 666th Meeting, 1 Mar. 1957, para. 1, p. 1275.
[34] Ibid., para. 28, p. 1277.
[35] Department of State, *Middle East*, pp. 322–3.

to Gaza mainly to show that, despite U.N.E.F., Egypt still held
its legal rights there. Although deploring the timing, Hammarskjold saw no legal grounds for refusing. The Israelis strenuously
objected to the U.N. 'surrender' to Nasser, but rejected the proposal that U.N.E.F.'s status be strengthened by allowing it to be
deployed on both sides of the armistice line, the Israeli as well as
the Egyptian. In the next days, Hammarskjold in personal talks
with Nasser worked out a *modus vivendi* for U.N.E.F. to remain
in Gaza and at the Gulf of Aqaba, without Egyptian troops being
there.[36]

The interposition of U.N.E.F. between Egyptian and Israeli
forces on the armistice demarcation line in Gaza and in Sharm el-
Sheikh was done under the general mandate. It represented Hammarskjold's understanding of the mood of the Assembly—that
U.N.E.F. should continue to act as a buffer between the opposing
armies while the parties searched for a lasting settlement. The
Assembly adjourned, after expressing its gratitude to the Secretary-
General for his efforts in defusing the crisis, but without making
any provision for negotiations between Egypt and Israel or taking
other measures designed to facilitate a political settlement.

3. THE NEW REGIME FOR THE CANAL

During March, as the completion of the salvage operation drew
near, the question of the Canal regime arose once more. On 18
March, Egypt circulated a draft on the subject, stating that a more
detailed statement would be issued later. The draft was discussed
and commented on by the United States and other users and by
the Secretary-General. Egypt insisted that tolls be paid to the
Egyptian Canal Authority. According to President Nasser, the only
guarantee for the users would be Egypt's promise to protect their
rights under the 1888 Constantinople Convention on freedom of
navigation. An Egyptian official also stated that the blockade
against Israel in the Canal would be continued.

The United States seemed resigned to obtaining the best arrangement possible without putting pressure on Egypt. Dulles noted
that 'the United States has no pressures to bring to bear in terms
of military threats or boycotts of the Canal or the like'. On 17
April, the President backed away from any demand for international control or ownership of the Canal and said the United
States was willing to accept 'operation of the Canal under the Six

[36] Urquhart, pp. 213–17.

Principles previously adopted by the United Nations'.[37] Direct discussions held between the United States and Egypt achieved only limited results.

On 24 April Egypt sent a letter to the Secretary-General setting forth its final position on the management and operation of the Suez Canal, which made several concessions to the West.

1. Egypt repeated its resolve to 'respect the terms and spirit of the Constantinople Convention of 1888'.

2. Tolls would be fixed at the Company level, and would not be increased (by more than 1 per cent a year) except by agreement or arbitration.

3. 'The Canal would be operated ... by the autonomous Suez Canal Authority established by the Government of Egypt on 26 July 1956.' Egypt would welcome co-operation between the Authority and representatives of shipping and trade.

4. Egypt proposed international arbitration of complaints of discrimination or other violations of the Canal code.

5. Disputes over the meaning of the Constantinople Convention of 1888 would be referred to the International Court of Justice. Egypt would accept compulsory jurisdiction of the Court under Article 36 of its statute.

6. The Canal would be maintained and developed according to the programme previously established by the Company. Twenty-five per cent of the gross receipts of the Canal would be deposited in a fund to be used to develop the Canal.

7. Changes in the regulations could be challenged and submitted to an international arbitral tribunal.

Egypt further stated: 'This Declaration with the obligations therein constitutes an international instrument and will be deposited and registered with the Secretariat of the United Nations.'[38]

By May 1957, all states except Israel were again using the Canal.

[37] Department of State, *Middle East*, pp. 378, 382–4.
[38] U.N. GAOR, Supplements, 12th Session, 1–4, Doc. A/3574, 24 Apr. 1957, pp. 25–6.

VI

CONCLUSIONS

A SINGLE crisis like Suez hardly provides an adequate basis for generalizing about the role of law (legal norms, processes, claims, and institutions) in major controversies. Each case depends critically on its special circumstances. Suez is no exception. Yet a study of Suez does suggest some conclusions about the impact of law on such a crisis. Law was important, even if not ultimately controlling; it did substantially affect how the parties acted and interacted. One way to gain insights into the legal role is to compare the differences among the parties in their uses of law and in its impact on them. How did they relate their objectives to the legal order? For what purposes did they use law? In what ways did law influence specific actions and their consequences? To what extent was law more effective for some purposes and under some conditions than others? How were the instrumentalities of international order affected?

1

That law should have played a significant role at all needs explaining. After all, the roots of the crisis lay deep in intense political rivalries and tensions in the Middle East: Nasser's drive to eject foreign influence and to enhance his own; Britain's tenacious effort to preserve its interests and traditional role in the region; the rebellion in Algeria; the Arab–Israeli conflict; the Soviet drive to expand into the Middle East, and the struggle of the U.S. (and its allies) to counter it; and the local rivalries among Arab states. Each major party rated the stakes highly, and some considered them as vital. Specific events—the Suez Base Agreement, the Baghdad Pact, the supply of arms, the Aswan Dam, the Gaza Raid, or the Suez takeover—all were seen as episodes in these larger contests. Beyond the immediate dispute, each party was concerned with future positions, relations, or capacities in the region, and with shaping them in conformity with its objectives. These objectives diverged, among other things, in how they could be related to legal norms and the legal order.

For differing reasons, the United States, Nasser (and the U.S.S.R.), and the users were convinced that law could be an effective instrumentality in achieving their objectives. That inevitably made law a key factor in the crisis.

The United States. The U.S. stress on law was based on both general and specific reasons. One of its major purposes was to maintain and strengthen the legal order embodied in the U.N. Charter, and two obligations in particular: (1) to refrain from the threat or use of force, and (2) to settle disputes by peaceful means in conformity with the principles of justice and international law. Eisenhower and Dulles were, it seems to me, genuinely convinced that these complementary principles were essential foundations for international order, and they sought to apply them to the various phases of the crisis. Critics have contended that Eisenhower and Dulles disregarded these principles at other times such as in Lebanon or Quemoy Matsu, or Guatemala. But they undoubtedly considered these as cases of collective defence justified under Article 51 of the Charter, or of civil war, and therefore wholly different from Suez.

In the Suez case, their support for these U.N. principles was reinforced by major practical and political factors. The basic U.S. interest in the region was to preserve stability and minimize Soviet penetration as far as possible. Eisenhower was convinced that the use of force could not impose a viable Canal regime or unseat Nasser, that it would alienate the Arabs and other new nations, and that it would facilitate Soviet penetration of the region. Thus U.S. interests would be jeopardized by Anglo-French intervention (or the Israeli attack). Yet while he considered the Anglo-French reaction excessive, Eisenhower recognized the critical interests of the major users in reliable access to the Canal and in its efficient operation, as well as the danger posed by Nasser's unconstrained control.

Consequently, the U.S. sought to isolate or separate the Canal dispute from the political rivalries, to avoid any resort to force, and to negotiate a solution providing adequate safeguards for the users. Adherence to the U.N. principles offered the best basis for this course and for rallying support for it. For this approach to succeed, however, the U.S. not only had to apply U.N. principles in its own key decisions, but it also had to induce compliance with them by the other parties, especially Britain, France, and Egypt. In so far as these principles influenced the course of the controversy, it was largely due to U.S. pressure. The other parties, however, also sought to utilize legal norms and institutions for their purposes.

Egypt. It was ironic that the other party best situated to use legal norms and agencies to serve its interests was Egypt. And Nasser showed impressive ability to do so in his handling of the crisis. Judging by the record, he must have had skilled legal advice at each stage. He benefited, of course, from the U.S. policy, but he took full advantage of the opportunities it offered.

Since his political purpose had been achieved by the abrupt seizure of the Canal Company, his concern in the crisis was mainly defensive—to retain control of the Canal under conditions which would not impair his political gains and to protect himself against forceful reaction. He counted on Soviet support in various forms. And apparently he hoped to appeal to public opinion in the major democracies and to arouse sympathy and support among leaders of the developing nations. Specifically, his aims were (1) to reassure the Canal users regarding access to the Canal or its normal operation; (2) to block any resort to force by Britain or France; and (3) to mobilize support for U.N. assistance in the case of any attack.

As Nasser recognized, law and legal norms were well suited to bolster this defensive strategy. From the start, as has been seen, he sought to define the controversy in legal terms and to lay out a persuasive legal foundation for his position. Thus the nationalization conformed to legal norms, providing compensation for the Canal Company. The Convention of 1888 provided a ready-made basis for Nasser to reassure users and to identify himself as law-abiding, without abandoning the legal premiss for denying Israeli use. The U.N. Charter offered the ground for branding as provocative the Anglo-French actions in blocking funds, withholding tolls, mobilizing forces, and withdrawing pilots, and for denouncing as unlawful any resort to forceful action. General readiness to negotiate and calls for wider conferences would blunt the rejection of the London Conference, the Eighteen-Power Proposal, and S.C.U.A. And after the attack in October, U.N. procedures and principles could be used to mobilize support for the withdrawals, with minimum concessions by Egypt.

U.S.S.R. The Soviet objective was primarily to use the crisis to enhance its position and influence in the Middle East at the expense of the West. Hence the U.S.S.R. sought to present itself as the reliable supporter of Egypt (and the Arabs) against the Western 'imperialists'. Backing Nasser's legal position was an effective way to carry out this strategy, without committing itself to assistance beyond its actual capacity. This the Soviet Union did from the start, in the London Conference, in the U.N., and in its propaganda. Its missile-rattling and threats of 'volunteers' after the attack were carefully timed to avoid any risk of becoming operational. Moreover, it was not at all deterred from its espousal of U.N. principles to oppose the Suez attack by its own concurrent suppression of the revolt in Hungary. Indeed, playing up the Suez events and the resulting Western confusion diverted attention from the Hungarian tragedy and reduced the risks of a Western reaction.

Canal Users. The Canal users as a group also wanted a peaceful solution, though their objectives otherwise conflicted with Nasser's. They needed reliable operation of the Canal: no discrimination, efficient management, fair tolls, adequate maintenance, and expansion for growing needs as well as safeguards against political leverage by Egypt. In the past, these interests had been protected not only by the Convention of 1888 but by the presence of British troops and by the Company as a buffer. With British troops gone, and the Egyptian Canal agency replacing the Company, the users were left with only the Egyptian promise to comply with the Convention of 1888.

To buttress the Egyptian promises, they therefore wanted some stronger structure to protect against violations of the Convention of 1888 or abuses not covered by the Convention. Clearly, such safeguards could take various forms, but the essential features must be effective constraint on unilateral Egyptian control and an adequate voice for users on such questions as tolls, maintenance, and expansion. Thus their goal was to improve the legal regime for the Canal, and to do so by peaceful means, if only to avoid disruption of its operation.

For that result, Nasser would have to be persuaded to accept a curtailment of the autonomy of the Canal authority and structural safeguards against abuse. In practice, he had a long-term interest in inducing users and potential users to plan on indefinite dependence on the Canal; otherwise, they might develop alternatives which could reduce its revenues or growth. Yet Nasser did not seem to recognize this reality in the early stages of the crisis.

Thus although the U.S. and ordinary users on one hand, and Nasser and the U.S.S.R., on the other, were at one in pressing to prevent resort to force and in invoking the U.N. Charter to that end, they diverged widely in their conceptions about the nature of an acceptable solution. Tactically, in devising proposals, the U.S. was also preoccupied with the necessity of inducing the U.K. and France to refrain from force, whereas Nasser apparently saw no need to respond to the user demands for institutional safeguards.

2

Conversely, the U.K., France, and Israel, while ultimately agreeing to collaborate in the use of force against Egypt, differed profoundly in their objectives and in their relation to legal norms and institutions.

United Kingdom and France. As Britain and France saw it, their struggle with Nasser could not be fitted into the context of international law. It was at bottom a political contest. Their perspective took the dispute outside the legal sphere; their objectives could not be attained by legal means. That fact was at the root of their divergences with the United States.

Britain and France were troubled primarily by the erosion of their historic positions in the Middle East, especially in the context of their general decline in relative power. The basic causes of those changes were mainly indigenous forces, including awakened nationalism, new aspirations, old resentments, and the weakening of traditional or feudal regimes. Nasser did not create these forces, but he did exploit them by subversion and propaganda. The Algerian revolt would have gone on, and British influences would have declined anyhow, but Nasser's activities were bound to exacerbate the British and French frustrations. Neither country was ready to accept its loss of position without resistance. For each, Nasser became a symbol and an apparent source of its difficulties.

The seizure of the Canal was only the last straw. If Nasser 'got away with it', his capacity to undermine Anglo-French interest would be vastly strengthened. With control of the Canal, he would be a threat to the vital oil supply route; and as an Arab nationalist hero, his ability to influence or disrupt regimes friendly to Britain or France would be greatly enhanced. Thus Nasser himself was the real problem.

That problem could not be met by taking issue with him over

safeguards for the Canal. The effort of Eisenhower and Dulles to isolate the Suez dispute from those wider concerns was misguided. It ignored the lessons of the thirties, that it was unwise to resist the salami tactics of dictators piecemeal or to debate their technical propriety.

For the British (and the French) the only satisfactory answer was to discredit or depose Nasser. Anything less would be a triumph for him and would hasten the ultimate catastrophe for their wider interests. To deflate or unseat Nasser would require force. Certainly he would not consent to reverse himself or step down; legal or peaceful means—negotiation or U.N. resolutions —would ultimately be futile in dealing with the fundamental problem. If the British and French had been free to act independently, they would almost surely have given Nasser an ultimatum and then moved to destroy him.

That they could not do. Before any resort to force, they needed time to ready their military forces, and to gain U.S. support to supply oil (if it led to closing the Canal or cutting pipelines) and to stand off Soviet threats. With the U.S. firmly opposing use of force, and the Labour Party taking a similar line at home, Britain (and France) reluctantly adapted to these pressures but did not change their basic objectives. The task was to manage the crisis so as: (1) to show the futility of peaceful means and to justify British and French self-help, or (2) to provoke Nasser into some step which could provide an adequate pretext for a forceful response.

In consequence, Britain and France were put under severe constraints in pursuing their real goal. They could not assert it publicly but were compelled to focus on the Canal issue and to justify their demands regarding the Canal in terms which would appear legitimate to others. And that ran the risk that the Canal dispute might be resolved, depriving them of their pretext for settling scores with Nasser. Indeed, when a Canal solution looked imminent, they ultimately developed another concept for collusion with Israel in order to justify force.

Israel. While Israel gladly co-operated with Britain and France in the attack on Egypt, its position differed radically from theirs in both its bases and its objectives. Israel considered that its resort to self-help was justified by repeated violations of its legal rights and the failure to obtain redress from the institutions in the international system. Israel's aim was not to subvert the legal order but to make its operation more effective for the future.

For Israel, Egypt's denial of the Canal violated the 1888 Convention, the armistice terms, and the 1951 resolution of the Security Council calling on Egypt to end the blockade; and its blockage of the Gulf of Aqaba, giving access to the Israeli port at Eilat, disregarded its status as an international waterway, at great cost to Israel's economy. Fedayeen raids, with their steady toll in Israel, were contrary to the armistice and the U.N. Charter; neither the U.N. nor harsh Israeli reprisals could stop them. Against this background the Soviet rearming of Egypt seemed a serious threat to Israel's security.

The Israeli leaders undoubtedly felt that the U.N. and its members were ignoring Israel's rightful claims. No one had followed up the 1951 Security Council resolution; the Soviet Union had indeed vetoed a second resolution in 1954. Nor was anyone backing freedom of passage through the Gulf of Aqaba. And U.N. resolutions, after armistice violations, more often than not condemned Israel because of the severity of its reprisals. Thus the Israelis claimed the right to self-defence under Article 51, in order to destroy the bases for the fedayeen raids rather than merely to retaliate after the event.

Despite the violations of Israel's rights, it was still hard to square its resort to force with the provisions of the Charter. And in practical terms, Israel weakened its position by the collusion with France and Britain. Their case for self-help was less clear; they had not exhausted efforts for a peaceful solution; and in any case, their action was based on the flimsy pretext of peacekeeping. These differences certainly influenced the outcomes.

3

In the first phase of the crisis, the parties sought to utilize law and legal norms in various ways for their differing purposes. The combined effect of the U.S. and Egyptian strategies and the interests of most Canal users was to focus the dispute on the Canal regime and to compel the parties to frame and justify their positions in legal terms. For their separate reasons both the U.S. and Egypt were seeking to restrain the British and French from resorting to force. But at the same time, the U.S. was trying to induce Nasser to negotiate a modified Canal regime offering more effective safeguards for the users, while Nasser was resisting any change in Egyptian control, and the British and French were attempting to show the futility of peaceful means for resolving the crisis.

In pursuing their objectives, all parties were drawing on the same legal materials: the Convention and Concessions, the U.N. Charter and general international law. The other means available to the U.S. for resolving the crisis were limited. The Anglo-French need for U.S. support or acquiescence in any use of force did give potential leverage against its precipitate use. But U.S. influence on Nasser was not so great. Economic pressures, such as freezing foreign balances, withholding Canal tolls, or suspending aid, were not very effective, at least in the short run. Negotiations might well have been encouraged by a vague risk of force in the background, whatever its propriety under the U.N. Charter. In some of his later press and U.N. statements Dulles tried to suggest such a risk existed in the absence of a Canal settlement, but the Anglo-French attitude compelled him to disavow any such threat.

In stressing the legality of his position, Nasser enjoyed one special advantage. Unlike the users, who wanted a new Canal regime, Nasser could succeed by merely keeping the situation unchanged. Doubtless his stand would not have constrained Britain and France if the U.S. had not opposed force. Still it contributed to Eisenhower and Dulles's perception of the situation and of the appropriate responses, and made it much harder for the British and French to bring the dispute to a head. Meanwhile Nasser counted on his assurances and the passage of time to defuse the crisis and remove risks of forceful action, as the Canal continued to operate without interruption and the first sense of outrage was dissipated.

For the U.S., the U.N. Charter provided a defensible ground for resisting Anglo-French use of force. By invoking the U.N. principles, Eisenhower and Dulles could readily communicate the U.S. position and its rationale both to domestic opinion and to allied officials and publics. By relating the Suez issue to loyalty to the U.N., they could generate domestic and foreign understanding and support more easily than by detailed analysis of the specific controversy. Moreover, by identifying their stand with broader commitments, they conveyed to the British and French leaders the strength of their opposition to use of force. And by its position towards its allies, the U.S. also enhanced its credibility with other users (especially among the newer nations) which was critical for the other branch of its policy towards Nasser.

But if the U.S. and Nasser used the U.N. Charter in parallel ways to restrain force, the parties invoked the Convention of 1888 for conflicting purpose. For Nasser, the Convention was invaluable as a means for asserting his intentions to operate the Canal normally. By promising compliance with its terms, he sought to reassure users that the Convention would continue to apply under the new regime, and that it should be sufficient protection against abuse. The concern of many of the users was deeper than Nasser realized, however; as the London Conference showed, even the newer countries were uneasy that he might exploit control of the Canal for leverage when it suited his purposes.

The U.S. and the users sought to utilize the Convention to put pressure on Nasser to negotiate additional safeguards. For this purpose, it was essential to mobilize the users, especially the developing nations, and to concert on a joint scheme for added safeguards. Yet establishing a legal basis for restricting Egyptian control of the Canal posed some difficulty. The claim that the takeover violated the 'system' established by the 1888 Convention was tenuous. After all, by its terms the Convention was not limited to the duration of the Concession; the effect of the seizure of the Company was essentially to anticipate what was destined to occur in twelve years. Of course, the abrupt termination of the Concession without notice was much more disturbing for the users than would have been an anticipated expiration, which would have allowed them time to arrange for more secure safeguards or to plan alternatives.

The real need of the users was to make new law. The Canal had become a vital waterway for much of the world. Given this dependence, a strong case could be made that the Canal was an international utility that should not be under the unregulated control of a single state which might exploit it for its own purposes. The United States, however, was deterred from espousing this general ground because of its potential application to the Panama Canal, which the U.S. was not willing to transfer to an international agency in view of its national strategic importance. Thus, the United States (and the users) had to rest the Suez case specifically on the Convention of 1888, and to assert that the treaty status of the Panama Canal was not analogous.

In consequence, the legal position of the users was not a wholly convincing basis for the remedy they sought. Even if shortening the life of the Company by twelve years was unlawful, that was a weak ground for insisting that Nasser should agree to institutional safe-guards in perpetuity. Nevertheless, basing the demand for further safeguards on the Convention had one advantage. Since the Convention was the concrete expression of the users' interest in reliable operation of the Canal, it was a persuasive foundation for rallying support for better safeguards against its unilateral abuse.

There was still the problem of defining just what kind of Canal regime would be satisfactory. Most users, including the U.S., would probably have accepted a system based on continued Egyptian operation, as long as it was subject to institutional controls assuring a significant user role Such a compromise, however, conflicted with the Anglo-French objective of undermining or humiliating Nasser and with their tactical aim of showing the futility of peaceful efforts. The proposal for an international Canal agency seemed to meet their criteria—since Nasser could not agree to it without reversing the nationalization entirely and discrediting himself. But to be doubly sure, they limited the discretion of Menzies's mission to consider alternatives. Conversely, at this stage, Nasser seemed unwilling to make any concession on the Canal regime; he ignored the more modest Spanish proposal (for user members on the Egyptian Canal Board) and submitted no alternatives.

The S.C.U.A. proposal displayed the same cross-purposes. While Dulles's aim was to promote negotiation, Eden tried to convert S.C.U.A. into a provocation and pretext for force, as had been done by the exercise of other 'legal' rights in blocking funds, paying tolls to the Company, calling off the European pilots. Any interruption or denial of use of the Canal might justify forcible measures, in which Eisenhower might have to acquiesce. Each 'escape' by Dulles was a frustrating defeat for this strategy.

The process reached its climax with the U.N. appeal, which Eden and Mollet viewed as the last step in 'exhausting' peaceful means. The private talks among Fawzi, Lloyd, and Pineau, however, seemed to vindicate the U.S. strategy. Fawzi appeared to be seeking a practical compromise with significant user safeguards regarding the level of tolls, the financing of development, discrimination, and so forth. By then Nasser may have come to realize the necessity for accepting some further protection for the Canal users to assure their continued dependence, or he may have been merely yielding to Arab and Soviet pressures. The British and French also felt compelled to engage in these talks, although their participation may have been only a 'cover', as Pineau's attitude suggests, whatever Lloyd intended. After all, the French and Israelis had worked out the plans for collusion, and Eden was probably already aware of them, and about to agree finally to take part. That would explain the Anglo-French insistence on a resolution ignoring the private talks and so offensive to Nasser as to assure a Soviet veto. Strictly speaking, a Canal settlement would not have prevented the Anglo-French collusion with the Israelis, since its pretext was a separate 'peacekeeping' action. But in practice it would surely have upset the plans.

4

After the resort to force, the course and outcome of the crisis were also substantially shaped by legal factors.

For the British and French, the influence was perverse. The decision to dress up the Anglo-French intervention as 'peacekeeping' was, of course, dictated by the desire to provide a cloak of 'legality'. It testified to the barrier which had been built up against resort to force on the basis of the Canal dispute. It was also an act of desperation. Since they could not persuade Eisenhower to resort to force, they hoped to compel his acquiescence by a *fait accompli.*

The 'legal' pretence interfered with the objectives. The claim of separating the combatants rang false when the Israelis were still not close to the Canal, and it became a transparent pretext when the British and French vetoed the Security Council Resolution. Yet acting out the pretence inhibited the early dispatch of forces by sea from Malta for a prompt landing in Egypt. Finally, the pretext of peacekeeping made the Anglo-French intervention vulnerable to the U.N. action in forming U.N.E.F. and deprived them of any basis for extracting a reformed Canal regime as a condition for withdrawal.

The contrast with Israel was striking. The U.N. General Assembly, led by the United States, lumped Israel with Britain and France, rejected its claim of self-help, and called for unconditional withdrawal of its forces along with theirs. Yet, in the course of its withdrawal, unlike Britain and France, Israel did obtain certain of its objectives. The Israelis insisted that it was wrong for the U.N. merely to restore the conditions which had given rise to the hostilities. The U.N. had an obligation to rectify the Egyptian violations of the armistice and the U.N. Charter, at the same time as it required withdrawal of Israeli forces. The General Assembly, the United States, and Hammarskjold demanded withdrawal before attending to the other issues. Despite this, the Israelis did manage to extract some relief with respect to the Gulf of Aqaba and the Gaza Strip.

Why were they able to be so? One reason, surely, was the awareness by the U.N. members and the Secretary-General that the U.N. had indeed neglected the violations to which Israel had been subjected. Of course, Israel was not without fault, especially in its disregard of the plight of the Palestinian refugees. But even so, the blockage of the Canal and of the Gulf of Aqaba as well as the continued fedayeen raids were indeed contrary to the rule of law. The Israeli demands were directly relevant to the original wrongs and to the provocation for the attack. Thus, its claim that the Gulf of Aqaba be recognized as an international waterway through which Israel and others were legally entitled to innocent passage could scarcely be denied by the United States. And it was hard to oppose the proposal to station U.N.E.F. units on the adjoining coast to oversee the Gulf, and in the Gaza Strip to separate the opposing sides, as the Israelis withdrew. No similar method could be applied to the Canal, and when it reopened, Egypt continued to deny access to Israel, with nothing done to correct it. Even so, for ten years Israel did gain two of the three points which had led it to undertake the military action in the first place.

Thus Israel did much better than Britain and France. In part, the British and French were hoist by their own pretext, which deprived them of any leverage in opposing withdrawal. Having based their intervention on stopping the fighting, they could not justify it after the Israel–Egypt ceasefire. While U.N.E.F. was a sop to their pretence, it gained them nothing for their real grievances either in safeguarding the Canal operation or in discrediting Nasser. Even if they had justified their attack by the Canal dispute, their case would have had two serious flaws. First, they could not have shown that Nasser had violated any clear legal obligations thus far, as the Israelis could. But secondly, at the U.N. before the attack, Nasser had shown readiness to explore added safeguards for the Canal, and he had agreed to further talks set for October 29 which were prevented by the attack.

These conditions were in direct contrast to the Israeli situation. Israel had based its attack on its actual legal grievances, though it stressed the fedayeen attacks mainly because they offered a ground for claiming self-defence under Article 51, which was less arguable for the denial of access to Canal and Gulf. In the later bargaining over withdrawal, therefore, Israel was in a much better position to exact partial remedies for specific violations.

This partial success was due largely to Israel's skilful use of law, especially in dealing with the U.S. Israel's argument that peace and justice were two sides of the same coin was consistent with the Charter principles as well as with Dulles's personal views. Its demands for equal treatment under the Charter and for not restoring the same conditions which had provoked the resort to force were plausible and hard to reject without some effort to meet them. Moreover, by resting its access to the Straits of Tiran on the general right under international law, Israel enabled the U.S. to commit itself to vindicating that right before Israeli withdrawal without seeming to undercut Hammarskjold or the United Nations. In theory, the same was true of the right to Canal passage, but the reality was quite different: it was clearly not feasible to invoke the threat of force under Article 51 for denial of the Canal as could be done in the case of forcible blockage of the Straits. The U.S. support on Gaza, though less explicit, was also valuable in assuring Israel regarding the U.N.E.F. role after its withdrawal. Yet despite obvious sympathy for Israel's predicament, Eisenhower finally used the full weight of U.S. pressure to secure its withdrawal on the basis of rather fragile safeguards against future violations of its rights.

As in his handling of the Canal dispute, Nasser showed skill in the second phase after the Israeli attack and the Anglo-French intervention, especially in his use of law to bolster his position. During the first stage he had managed not to alienate many U.N. members whose support was essential during the U.N. proceedings. He could take some credit for the U.N. outcome, even though the U.S. and the Secretary-General were mainly responsible for it. U.N.E.F. was a mixed blessing for Nasser, but the U.N. operation as a whole rescued Egypt from occupation by Britain, France, and Israel. Despite his heavy dependence on the U.N., Nasser largely succeeded in preserving his legal contention that the U.N.E.F. presence rested on Egyptian consent, though finally accepting the Secretary-General's 'good faith' formula. Thus even *in extremis*, Nasser was able to utilize legal doctrine to strengthen his position and to resist the pressures for greater concessions. In particular, he yielded nothing regarding the Canal in this stage. When it reopened, it was under a regime proclaimed unilaterally by Egypt.

Even so, the provisions for the Canal regime suggested that Nasser had grasped the role of legal norms and remedies in its operation. While hardly ideal, the system did provide for user participation in fixing tolls and regulations, and for impartial adjudication of certain types of disputes. Thus, at the end of the crisis, although Nasser had 'won' on most scores, he had partly to come to terms with the users' concern for reliability of the Canal, if only to serve Egypt's interests in keeping the Canal profitable. Yet, since his concessions regarding Canal operation and the stationing of U.N.E.F. could be presented as based on Egyptian consent, they did not impair his prestige or influence at home or in the region. *In toto*, the Suez episode probably enhanced Nasser's capacity for future subversion. The Anglo-French co-operation with Israel and their defeat certainly reduced their ability to counter him. And it is equally true that the U.N. was powerless to prevent Nasser's efforts to subvert and cow rival Arab states.

5

The crisis also had a major impact on the instruments of international law and order. It stimulated a significant political-legal invention in the creation of the United Nations Emergency Force. And Hammarskjold's handling of the affairs greatly enhanced the role of the Secretary-General.

That office is, of course, a creation of international law, deriving its authority from the United Nations Charter, itself a treaty. While the Charter sets out the duties of the Secretary-General in general terms, he is also to 'perform such other functions as are entrusted to him by the Security Council and the General Assembly (Article 98). Under that article, the General Assembly empowered the Secretary-General to plan, establish, and direct U.N.E.F. The idea for the Force was Lester Pearson's, and Dulles promptly backed it. The opportunity was created by the widespread sense that the United Nations must do something to stabilize the situation. But Hammarskjold, while initially sceptical, deserves the credit for developing the concept and making the force effective. Once involved, he performed the task with extraordinary skill, imagination, and speed, drawing on his great ingenuity in devising formulas for the legal and practical problems involved. In short, the formation of U.N.E.F. was a brilliant *tour de force* in the constructive development of international law and institutions. It reflected Hammarskjold's conception of law. He viewed law not 'as a construction of ideal patterns', but in an 'organic sense', as 'an institution which grows in response to felt necessities and within the limits set by historical conditions and human attitudes'.[1] The contribution that Hammarskjold made to the growth of international law and institutions through U.N.E.F. remains one of the most notable aspects both of the Suez affair and of his remarkable service as Secretary-General.

U.N.E.F. bolstered stability in the Middle East for ten years and provided a model for peacekeeping in the Congo and Cyprus. It was, however, a buffer between hostile forces, and did not resolve the deeper problems. Indeed, as U.N.E.F. shows starkly, the international community has much greater capacity to enforce peace or resist resort to force than to cope with the underlying sources of conflict.

In theory, at least, U.N.E.F. might have assumed the broader and more ambitious task. In November, sentiment in the Assembly for confronting the deeper issues of the Middle East seemed widespread. Hammarskjold defined U.N.E.F.'s function as helping to maintain quiet, and to 'secure compliance with the other terms in the cease-fire resolution of 2 November 1956'. Those 'other terms' included an injunction to reopen the Suez Canal and to restore secure freedom of navigation, and a provision urging the parties to the General Armistice Agreements to desist from raids and otherwise scrupulously to observe the armistice provisions. And the Assembly's general directives in its Resolution II of 2 February would have allowed the Secretary-General to expand the functions of U.N.E.F., if he had so desired.

There were several reasons why that was not done. The members contributing forces to U.N.E.F. did not view it as a vehicle for long-term settlements but as an emergency measure to separate the combatants and assure Israeli withdrawal. The tenuous legal basis for the force was doubtless a major factor in limiting what was attempted. Moreover, the course taken may well have reflected the maximum area of member consensus, mirroring the facts of international life. It was far easier to mobilize the U.N. to oppose invasion than to agree on solutions for the substantive issues. In practice, the members of the Assembly were content for Hammarskjold to focus on the immediate problems of ceasefire and withdrawal, and to shelve the U.S. resolutions dealing with long-term

[1] Oscar Schachter, 'Dag Hammarskjold and the Relation of Law to Politics', Am. J. Int'l L., vol. 56, no. 1 (Jan. 1962), pp. 1, 7 (and see page 4).

problems. Once the French, British, and Israeli forces had with-drawn completely, the U.N. delegates breathed a collective sigh of relief, leaving U.N.E.F. to patrol the armistice line between Israel and Egypt and to keep Egyptian guns from threatening the Straits of Tiran.

These tendencies were strongly reinforced by the insistence of the U.N., the U.S., and the Secretary-General that the withdrawal of forces must precede any effort to resolve the longer-term prob-lems in the Middle East. This priority was intended to deny the attacker any benefits from using force, but it deprived the U.N. of any leverage in settling the substantive problems and relegated them to the back seat.

Was it necessary to postpone taking up the causes of the hostili-ties until after withdrawal? In the Suez situation, it does not seem so. Of course, in a case of naked aggression, the entire focus should be on throwing back the aggressor and rescuing the victim. But the Arab–Israeli case was more complex: over an extended period one party (or both) had been engaged in violating important rights of the other, by force or threat of force, and international machinery did not provide effective relief. Under these conditions, an attempt at self-help, even if not condoned, poses the question as to how to proceed towards a just solution. When the victim has to some degree provoked the attack, he cannot claim com-pletely 'clean hands'. If the international community comes to his rescue, should it not consider the situation in its entirety? Why should it not at least require the acceptance of measures to pre-vent future violations as a condition of assistance? Or even better, use the occasion to find more basic solutions?

By this standard, as already indicated, Britain and France would not have been in the same posture as Israel. But as between Egypt and Israel, the international community might well have made assistance to Egypt dependent on the resolution of the problems of Aqaba, the Canal, the raids, and related issues.

Actually, the strict doctrine was modified in this direction by practical actions. The Secretary-General used the threat of with-holding U.N.E.F. to persuade Nasser to accept the 'good faith' limitation on withdrawing his consent. The concessions ultimately made to the Israeli demands were hardly consistent with the rigid insistence on unconditional withdrawal. Even more significant was the aftermath of the Six Day War ten years later. The U.N. Secur-ity Council resolution adopted in November 1967 called for establishment of a just and lasting peace based on *both* (1) withdrawal of Israeli forces from occupied territories; and (2) recognition of the sovereignty and integrity of all States (including Israel) and their right to peace within secure borders; and it specifically called for settling the issues of the Canal, Aqaba, and refugees. In practical terms, withdrawal was linked with settling the other sources of Arab–Israeli conflict. The 1967 events can be traced to the inadequacy of the 1957 solution; and the 1967 resolution is a *de facto* change in the theory adopted in 1957. Admittedly, such an approach tends to legitimize resort to self-help and could tempt parties to use force in order to coerce concessions. On balance, however, it seems justified in a proper case.

6

How then should the role of international law be appraised in the Suez Crisis? The criterion cannot be whether unlawful action or violence or conflict were prevented. No domestic legal system is expected to achieve that. It aims to reduce illegal conduct and violence to manageable proportions and to facilitate orderly handling of controversies. To a large extent, the domestic legal order relies on the fact that conformity with the legal norms and processes serves the interests of the vast majority and enlists their voluntary support and co-operation. International law, with limited means of enforcement, depends even more on engaging the interests of states to achieve effectiveness even to a more modest degree. Inevitably other factors often have greater influence on outcomes in international conflict.

Taken by itself, the outcome of the Suez crisis could be viewed as a qualified success for international law. Although the British, French, and Israelis were not prevented from ultimately resorting to force, they were compelled to withdraw in conformity with the U.N. Charter. The British and the French gained nothing from their intervention; and the Israelis only partial remedies for Egyptian violations. Although neither the parties nor the U.N. achieved an agreed settlement of the Canal dispute, Nasser's unilateral regime took some account of the users' interests by providing certain legal safeguards. And although U.N.E.F. did not solve the basic issues, it dampened conflict and enhanced stability in the Middle East for a decade.

The outcome was substantially influenced by the ways in which the major parties related their objectives to the legal order, and utilized law in pursuing them. Legal norms, processes, and institutions served not only as a constraint, but as a means to communicate objectives and intentions, to indicate acceptance of obligations and limitations, to identify common positions, and to rally support among diverse groups. In other words, law was made operative largely to the extent that the parties conformed to it or utilized it as an instrument of policy for demands, defence, or definition of positions.

It would be a mistake, however, to extrapolate from even the limited success of the Suez crisis. It had certain features critical for the outcome, which may be absent in other controversies. Most important was the fact that the U.S. and the Soviet Union for their separate reasons were both committed to opposing resort to force. With their parallel support, the U.N. applied constraints to middle and smaller powers, not the superpowers. Indeed, at that very time, the Soviet Union itself was brutally suppressing the popular uprising in Hungary in total disregard of the U.N. And on later occasions, such as the Dominican affair, the U.S. actions were hard to square with the principles it supported in the Suez crisis.

Inevitably, the handling of the crisis and the role of law in it evoke diverse appraisals. Cynics can see it as a classic case of the strong imposing legal constraints on the weaker. 'Realists' can criticize the U.S. for pursuing misguided priorities based on illusions which led it to combine with its adversaries to humiliate its closest allies. The more hopeful may see it as half a loaf in an imperfect world.

APPENDIXES

1. DOCUMENTARY

1. Excerpt from Cable of Eden to Eisenhower (27 July 1956)
(from Eden, pp. 476–7)

This morning I have reviewed the whole position with my Cabinet colleagues and Chiefs of Staff. We are all agreed that we cannot afford to allow Nasser to seize control of the canal in this way, in defiance of international agreements. If we take a firm stand over this now we shall have the support of all the maritime powers. If we do not, our influence and yours throughout the Middle East will, we are all convinced, be finally destroyed.

The immediate threat is to the oil supplies to Western Europe, a great part of which flows through the canal.... If the canal were closed we should have to ask you to help us by reducing the amount which you draw from the pipeline terminals in the eastern Mediterranean and possibly by sending us supplementary supplies for a time from your side of the world.

It is, however, the outlook for the longer term which is more threatening. The canal is an international asset and facility, which is vital to the free world. The maritime powers cannot afford to allow Egypt to expropriate it and to exploit it by using the revenues for her own internal purposes irrespective of the interests of the canal and of the canal users....

We should not allow ourselves to become involved in legal quibbles about the rights of the Egyptian Government to national-ize what is technically an Egyptian company, or in financial arguments about their capacity to pay the compensation which they have offered. I feel sure that we should take issue with Nasser on the broader international grounds.

As we see it we are unlikely to attain our objectives by econ-omic pressures alone. I gather that Egypt is not due to receive any further aid from you. No large payments from her sterling balances here are due before January. We ought in the first in-stance to bring the maximum political pressure to bear on Egypt.

For this, apart from our own action, we should invoke the support of all the interested powers. My colleagues and I are convinced that we must be ready, in the last resort, to use force to bring Nasser to his senses. For our part we are prepared to do so. I have this morning instructed our Chiefs of Staff to prepare a military plan accordingly.

However, the first step must be for you and us and France to exchange views, align our policies and concert together how we can best bring the maximum pressure to bear on the Egyptian Government.

2. *Letter from Eisenhower to Eden (31 July 1956)*
(from Eisenhower, pp. 664–5)

Dear Anthony:

From the moment that Nasser announced nationalization of the Suez Canal Company, my thoughts have been constantly with you. Grave problems are placed before both our governments, although for each of us they naturally differ in type and character. Until this morning, I was happy to feel that we were approaching decisions as to applicable procedures somewhat along parallel lines, even though there were, as would be expected, important differences as to detail. But early this morning I received the messages, communicated to me through Murphy from you and Harold Macmillan, telling me on a most secret basis of your decision to employ force without delay or attempting any intermediate and less drastic steps.

We recognize the transcendent worth of the Canal to the free world and the possibility that eventually the use of force might become necessary in order to protect international rights. But we have been hopeful that through a Conference in which would be represented the signatories to the Convention of 1888, as well as other maritime nations, there would be brought about such pressures on the Egyptian government that the efficient operation of the Canal could be assured for the future.

For my part, I cannot over-emphasize the strength of my conviction that some such method must be attempted before action such as you contemplate should be undertaken. If unfortunately the situation can finally be resolved only by drastic means, there should be no grounds for belief anywhere that corrective measures

were undertaken merely to protect national or individual investors, or the legal rights of a sovereign nation were ruthlessly
flouted. A conference, at the very least, should have a great
educational effect throughout the world. Public opinion here and,
I am convinced, in most of the world, would be outraged should
there be a failure to make such efforts. Moreover, initial military
successes might be easy, but the eventual price might become far
too heavy.

I have given you my own personal conviction, as well as that
of my associates, as to the unwisdom even of contemplating the
use of military force at this moment. Assuming, however, that
the whole situation continued to deteriorate to the point where
such action would seem the only recourse, there are certain political facts to remember. As you realize, employment of United States
forces is possible only through positive action on the part of the
Congress, which is now adjourned but can be reconvened on my
call for special reasons. If those reasons should involve the issue
of employing United States military strength abroad, there would
have to be a showing that every peaceful means of resolving the
difficulty had previously been exhausted. Without such a showing, there would be a reaction that could very seriously affect our
peoples' feeling toward our Western Allies. I do not want to
exaggerate, but I assure you that this could grow to such an in-
tensity as to have the most far-reaching consequences.

I realize that the messages from both you and Harold stressed
that the decision taken was already approved by the government
and was firm and irrevocable. But I personally feel sure that the
American reaction would be severe and that the great areas of the
world would share that reaction. On the other hand, I believe we
can marshal that opinion in support of a reasonable and concilia-
tory, but absolutely firm, position. So I hope that you will consent
to reviewing this matter once more in its broadest aspects. It is
for this reason that I have asked Foster to leave this afternoon to
meet with your people tomorrow in London.

I have given you here only a few highlights in the chain of
reasoning that compels us to conclude that the step you contemplate should not be undertaken until every peaceful means of protecting the rights and the livelihood of great portions of the world
had been thoroughly explored and exhausted. Should these means
fail, and I think it is erroneous to assume in advance that they
needs must fail, then world opinion would understand how ear-

nestly all of us had attempted to be just, fair and considerate, but that we simply could not accept a situation that would in the long run prove disastrous to the prosperity and living standards of every nation whose economy depends directly or indirectly upon East-West shipping.

With warm personal regard—and with earnest assurances of my continuing respect and friendship.

As ever,
DE

3. Cable from Eden to Eisenhower (27 August 1956) (from Eden, pp. 504–6)

This is a message to thank you for all the help Foster has given. Though I could not be at the Conference myself, I heard praise on all sides for the outstanding quality of his speeches and his constructive leadership. He will tell you how things have gone. It was, I think, a remarkable achievement to unite eighteen nations on an agreed statement of this clarity and force.

Before he left, Foster spoke to me of the destructive efforts of the Russians at the Conference. I have been giving some thought to this and I would like to give you my conclusions.

I have no doubt that the Bear is using Nasser, with or without his knowledge, to further his immediate aims. These are, I think, first to dislodge the West from the Middle East, and second to get a foothold in Africa so as to dominate that continent in turn. In this connection I have seen a reliable report from someone who was present at the lunch which Shepilov gave for the Arab Ambassadors. There the Soviet claim was that they "only wanted to see Arab unity in Asia and Africa and the abolition of all foreign bases and exploitation. An agreed unified Arab nation must take its rightful place in the world."

This policy is clearly aimed at Wheelus Field and Habbaniya, as well as at our Middle East oil supplies. Meanwhile the Communist bloc continue their economic and political blandishments towards the African countries which are already independent. Soon they will have a wider field for subversion as our colonies, particularly in the West, achieve self-government. All this makes me more than ever sure that Nasser must not be allowed to get away with it this time. We have many friends in the Middle East

and in Africa and others who are shrewd enough to know where
the plans of a Nasser or a Musaddiq would lead them. But they
will not be strong enough to stand against the power of the mobs
if Nasser wins again. The firmer the front we show together, the
greater the chance that Nasser will give way without the need for
any resort to force. That is why we were grateful for your policy
and Foster's expression of it at the Conference. It is also one of
the reasons why we have to continue our military preparations
in conjunction with our French allies.

We have been examining what other action could be taken if
Nasser refuses to negotiate on the basis of the London Conference.
There is the question of the dues. The Dutch and the Germans
have already indicated that they will give support in this respect.
The Dutch may even be taking action in the next few days. Then
there is the question of currency and economic action. We are
studying these with your people and the French in London and
will be sending our comments soon. It looks as though we shall
have a few days until Nasser gives Menzies his final reply. After
that we should be in a position to act swiftly. Selwyn Lloyd is
telegraphing to Foster about tactics, particularly in relation to
United Nations.

Meanwhile I thought I should set out some of our reflections
on the dangerous situation which still confronts us. It is certainly
the most hazardous that our country had known since 1940.

I was so glad to see such excellent photographic testimony of
your growing health and abounding energy. That is the very best
news for us all.

4. Letter from Eisenhower to Eden (2 September 1956)
(from Eisenhower, pp. 666–8)

Dear Anthony:
    I am grateful for your recent letter, and especially for your kind
words on the role of the United States during the London Conference on the Suez Canal. I share your satisfaction at the large
number of nations which thought as we do about the future operation of the Canal. In achieving this result we have set in motion
a force which I feel will be very useful to us—the united and
clearly expressed opinion of the majority users of the Suez waterway and of those nations most dependent upon it. This will exert

a pressure which Nasser can scarcely ignore. From Foster I know that this accomplishment is due in no small measure to the expert leadership exhibited by Selwyn Lloyd as Chairman of the Conference, and to the guidance which he received from you.

As for the Russians, it is clear that they sought, at London, to impede the consolidation of a majority point of view, and to generate an atmosphere in the Near East which would make it impossible for Nasser to accept our proposals. I entirely agree with you that the underlying purpose of their policy in this problem is to undermine the Western position in the Near East and Africa, and to weaken the Western nations at home. We must never lose sight of this point.

Now that the London Conference is over, our efforts must be concentrated on the successful outcome of the conversations with Nasser. This delicate situation is going to require the highest skill, not only on the part of the five-nation Committee but also on the part of our Governments. I share your view that it is important that Nasser be under no misapprehension as to the firm interest of the nations primarily concerned with the Canal in safeguarding their rights in that waterway.

As to the possibility of later appeal to the United Nations, we can envisage a situation which would require UN consideration and of course there should be no thought of military action before the influences of the UN are fully explored. However, and most important, we believe that, before going to the UN, the Suez Committee of Five should first be given full opportunity to carry out the course of action agreed upon in London, and to gauge Nasser's intentions.

If the diplomatic front we present is united and is backed by the overwhelming sentiment of our several peoples, the chances should be greater that Nasser will give way without the need for any resort to force. This belief explains our policy at the Conference and also explains the statement which I gave out through Foster after I got back from San Francisco and had a chance to talk fully with him.

I am afraid, Anthony, that from this point onward our views on this situation diverge. As to the use of force or the threat of force at this juncture, I continue to feel as I expressed myself in the letter Foster carried to you some weeks ago. Even now military preparations and civilian evacuation exposed to public view seem to be solidifying support for Nasser which has been shaky in many important quarters. I regard it as indispensable that if we are to proceed solidly together to the solution of this problem, public opinion in our several countries must be overwhelming in its support. I must tell you frankly that American public opinion flatly rejects the thought of using force, particularly when it does not seem that every possible peaceful means of protecting our vital interests has been exhausted without result. Moreover, I gravely doubt we could here secure Congressional authority even for the lesser support measures for which you might have to look to us.

I really do not see how a successful result could be achieved by forcible means. The use of force would, it seems to me, vastly increase the area of jeopardy. I do not see how the economy of Western Europe can long survive the burden of prolonged military operations, as well as the denial of Near East oil. Also the peoples of the Near East and of North Africa and, to some extent, of all of Asia and all of Africa, would be consolidated against the West to a degree which, I fear, could not be overcome in a generation and, perhaps not even in a century particularly having in mind the capacity of the Russians to make mischief. Before such action were undertaken, all our peoples should unitedly understand that there were no other means available to protect our vital rights and interests.

We have two problems, the first of which is the assurance of permanent and efficient operation of the Suez Canal with justice to all concerned. The second is to see that Nasser shall not grow as a menace to the peace and vital interests of the West. In my view, these two problems need not and possibly cannot be solved simultaneously and by the same methods, although we are exploring further means to this end. The first is the most important for the moment and must be solved in such a way as not to make the second more difficult. Above all, there must be no grounds for our several peoples to believe that anyone is using the Canal difficulty as an excuse to proceed forcibly against Nasser. And we have friends in the Middle East who tell us they would like to see Nasser's deflation brought about. But they seem unanimous in feeling that the Suez is not the issue on which to attempt to do this by force. Under those circumstances, because of the temper of their population, they say they would have to support Nasser even against their better judgment.

Seldom, I think, have we been faced by so grave a problem. For the time being we must, I think, put our faith in the processes already at work to bring Nasser peacefully to accept the solution along the lines of the 18-nation proposal. I believe that even though this procedure may fail to give the setback to Nasser that he so much deserves, we can better retrieve our position subsequently than if military force were hastily invoked.

Of course, our departments are looking into the implications of all future developments. In this they will keep in close touch with appropriate officials of your Government, as is my wish.

With warm regard,

As ever,
D.E.

5. *Excerpt from Letter from Eden to Eisenhower (6 September 1956)*
(from Eden, pp. 518–21)

Thank you for your message and writing thus frankly.

There is no doubt as to where we are agreed and have been agreed from the very beginning, namely that we should do everything we can to get a peaceful settlement. It is in this spirit that we favoured calling the twenty-two power conference and that we have worked in the closest co-operation with you about this business since. There has never been any question of our suddenly or without further provocation resorting to arms, while these processes were at work. In any event, as your own wide knowledge would confirm, we could not have done this without extensive preparation lasting several weeks.

This question of precautions has troubled me considerably and still does. I have not forgotten the riots and murders in Cairo in 1952, for I was in charge here at the time when Winston was on the high seas on his way back from the United States.

We are both agreed that we must give the Suez committee every chance to fulfil their mission. This is our firm resolve. If the committee and subsequent negotiations succeed in getting Nasser's agreement to the London proposals of the eighteen powers, there will be no call for force. But if the committee fails, we must have some immediate alternative which will show that Nasser is not going to get his way. In this connection we are attracted by Foster's suggestion, if I understand it rightly, for the running of the canal by the users in virtue of their rights under the 1888 Convention. We heard about this from our Embassy in Washington yesterday. I think that we could go along with this, provided that the intention was made clear by both of us immediately the Menzies mission finishes its work. But unless we can proceed with this, or something very like it, what should the next step be?

You suggest that this is where we diverge. If that is so I think that the divergence springs from a difference in our assessment of Nasser's plans and intentions. May I set out our view of the position.

In the nineteen-thirties Hitler established his position by a series of carefully planned movements. These began with occupation of the Rhineland and were followed by successive acts of aggression against Austria, Czechoslovakia, Poland and the West. His actions were tolerated and excused by the majority of the population of Western Europe. It was argued either that Hitler had committed no act of aggression against anyone, or that he was entitled to do what he liked in his own territory, or that it was impossible to prove that he had any ulterior designs, or that the Covenant of the League of Nations did not entitle us to use force and that it would be wiser to wait until he did commit an act of aggression.

In more recent years Russia has attempted similar tactics. The blockade of Berlin was to have been the opening move in a campaign designed at least to deprive the Western powers of their whole position in Germany. On this occasion we fortunately reacted at once with the result that the Russian design was never unfolded. But I am sure that you would agree that it would be wrong to infer from this circumstance that no Russian design existed.

Similarly the seizure of the Suez Canal is, we are convinced, the opening gambit in a planned campaign designed by Nasser to expel all Western influence and interests from Arab countries. He believes that if he can get away with this, and if he can successfully defy eighteen nations, his prestige in Arabia will be so great that he will be able to mount revolutions of young officers in Saudi Arabia, Jordan, Syria and Iraq. (We know that he is already preparing a revolution in Iraq, which is most stable and progressive.) These new Governments will in effect be Egyptian satellites if not Russian ones. They will have to place their united oil resources under the control of a United Arabia led by Egypt and under Russian influence. When that moment comes Nasser can deny oil to Western Europe and we here shall all be at his mercy.

There are some who doubt whether Saudi Arabia, Iraq and Kuwait will be prepared even for a time to sacrifice their oil revenues for the sake of Nasser's ambitions. But if we place ourselves in their position I think the dangers are clear. If Nasser says to them, "I have nationalized the Suez Canal. I have successfully defied eighteen powerful nations including the United States, I have defied the whole of the United Nations in the matter of the Israel blockade, I have expropriated all Western property. Trust me and withhold oil from Western Europe. Within six months or a year, the continent of Europe will be on its knees before you," will the Arabs not be prepared to follow this lead? Can we rely on them to be more sensible than were the Germans? Even if the Arabs eventually fall apart again as they did after the early Caliphs, the damage will have been done meanwhile.

In short we are convinced that if Nasser is allowed to defy the eighteen nations it will be a matter of months before revolution breaks out in the oil-bearing countries and the West is wholly deprived of Middle Eastern oil. In this belief we are fortified by the advice of friendly leaders in the Middle East.

The Iraquis are the most insistent in their warnings; both Nuri and the Crown Prince have spoken to us several times of the consequences of Nasser succeeding in his grab. They would be swept away. ... [ellipsis in Eden]

The difference which separates us today appears to be a difference of assessment of Nasser's plans and intentions and of the consequences in the Middle East of military action against him.

You may feel that even if we are right it would be better to wait until Nasser has unmistakably unveiled his intentions. But this was the argument which prevailed in 1936 and which we both rejected in 1948. Admittedly there are risks in the use of force against Egypt now. It is, however, clear that military intervention designed to reverse Nasser's revolutions in the whole continent would be a much more costly and difficult undertaking. I am very troubled, as it is, that if we do not reach a conclusion either way about the canal very soon one or other of these Eastern lands may be toppled at any moment by Nasser's revolutionary movements.

I agree with you that prolonged military operations as well as the denial of Middle East oil would place an immense strain on the economy of Western Europe. I can assure you that we are conscious of the burdens and perils attending military intervention. But if our assessment is correct, and if the only alternative is to allow Nasser's plans quietly to develop until this country and all Western Europe are held to ransom by Egypt acting at Russia's behest it seems to us that our duty is plain. We have many times led Europe in the fight for freedom. It would be an ignoble end to our long history if we accepted to perish by degrees.

6. Letter from Eisenhower to Eden (8 September 1956)
(from Eisenhower, pp. 669–71)

Dear Anthony:

Whenever, on any international question, I find myself differing even slightly from you, I feel a deep compulsion to re-examine my position instantly and carefully. But permit me to suggest that when you use phrases in connection with the Suez affair, like "ignoble end to our long history" in describing the possible future of your great country, you are making Nasser a much more important figure than he is.

We have a grave problem confronting us in Nasser's reckless adventure with the Canal, and I do *not* differ from you in your estimate of his intentions and purposes. The place where we apparently do not agree is on the probable effects in the Arab world of the various possible reactions by the Western world.

You seem to believe that any long, drawn-out controversy either within the 18-nation group or in the United Nations will inevitably make Nasser an Arab hero and seriously damage the prestige of Western Europe, including the United Kingdom, and that of the United States. Further you apparently believe that there would soon result an upheaval in the Arab nations out of which Nasser would emerge as the acknowledged leader of Islam. This, I think, is a picture too dark and is severely distorted.

I shall try to give you a somewhat different appraisal of the situation. First, let me say that my own conclusions are based to some degree upon an understanding of current Arab feeling that differs somewhat from yours. I believe that as this quarrel now stands before the world, we can expect the Arabs to rally firmly to Nasser's support in either of two eventualities.

The first of these is that there should be a resort to force without thoroughly exploring and exhausting every possible peaceful means of settling the issue, regardless of the time consumed, and when there is no evidence before the world that Nasser intends to do more than to nationalize the Canal Company. Unless it can be shown to the world that he is an actual aggressor, then I think all Arabs would be forced to support him, even though some of the ruling monarchs might very much like to see him toppled.

The second would be what seemed like a capitulation to Nasser and complete acceptance of his rule of the Canal traffic.

The use of military force against Egypt under present circumstances might have consequences even more serious than causing the Arabs to support Nasser. It might cause a serious misunderstanding between our two countries because I must say frankly that there is as yet no public opinion in this country which is prepared to support such a move, and the most significant public opinion that there is seems to think that the United Nations was formed to prevent this very thing.

It is for reasons such as these that we have viewed with some misgivings your preparations for mounting a military expedition against Egypt. We believe that Nasser may try to go before the United Nations claiming that these actions imply a rejection of the peaceful machinery of settling the dispute, and therefore may ask the United Nations to brand these operations as aggression.

At the same time, we do not want any capitulation to Nasser. We want to stand firmly with you to deflate the ambitious pretensions of Nasser and to assure permanent free and effective use of the Suez waterway under the terms of the 1888 Treaty.

It seems to Foster and to me that the result that you and I both want can best be assured by slower and less dramatic processes than military force. There are many areas of endeavor which are not yet fully explored because exploration takes time.

We can, for example, promote a semi-permanent organization of the user governments to take over the greatest practical amount of the technical problems of the Canal, such as pilotage, the organization of the traffic patterns, and the collection of dues to cover actual expenses. This organization would be on the spot and in constant contact with Egypt and might work out a *de facto* "coexistence" which would give the users the rights which we want.

There are economic pressures which, if continued, will cause distress in Egypt.

There are Arab rivalries to be exploited and which can be exploited if we do not make Nasser an Arab hero.

There are alternatives to the present dependence upon the Canal and pipelines which should be developed perhaps by more tankers, a possible new pipeline to Turkey and some possible rerouting of oil, including perhaps more from this hemisphere, particularly to European countries which can afford to pay for it in dollars.

Nasser thrives on drama. If we let some of the drama go out of the situation and concentrate upon the task of deflating him through slower but sure processes such as I described, I believe the desired results can more probably be obtained. Gradually it seems to me we could isolate Nasser and gain a victory which would not only be bloodless, but would be more far reaching in its ultimate consequences than could be anything brought about by force of arms. In addition, it would be less costly both now and in the future.

Of course, if during this process Nasser himself resorts to violence in clear disregard of the 1888 Treaty, then that would create a new situation and one in which he and not we would be violating the United Nations Charter.

I assure you we are not blind to the fact that eventually there may be no escape from the use of force. Our resolute purpose must be to create conditions of operation in which all users can have confidence. But to resort to military action when the world believes there are other means available for resolving the dispute would set in motion forces that could lead, in the years to come, to the most distressing results.

Obviously there are large areas of agreement between us. But in these exchanges directed towards differing methods I gain some clarification of the confusing and conflicting considerations that apply to this problem.

With warmest regard.

As ever your friend,

7. Letter from Mr. Hammarskjold to Dr. Fawzi concerning their talks with Mr. Selwyn Lloyd and M. Pineau in New York (24 October 1956)
(from Department of State, Middle East, pp. 127–30)

Dear Dr. Fawzi,

You will remember that at the end of the private talks on Suez, trying to sum up what I understood as being the sense of the discussion, I covered not only the 'requirements', later approved by the Security Council, but also, in a summary form, arrangements that had been discussed as possible means of meeting those requirements. However, time then proved insufficient for a satisfactory exploration of those arrrangements.

Before you left New York I raised with you the question of time and place for a resumption of the exploratory talks, in case the three Governments directly concerned would find that such further talks should be tried. As a follow up to these observations to which, so far, I have had no reactions either from you or from Mr. Selwyn Lloyd or Mr. Pineau, I would, for my own sake, wish to put on paper how I envisage the situation that would have to be studied at resumed exploratory talks, if they were to come about.

Again, what I do is not put out any proposals of my own, nor to try to formulate proposals made by you or any of the others. Just as I did at the end of the private talks in New York, I just wish in my own words, to try and spell out what are my conclusions from the—entirely non-committal—observations made in the course of the private talks where they did not fully cover the ground. Whether you approve of my phrasing or not, I feel that it would be valuable to know if, in your view, I have correctly interpreted the conclusions from the tentative thinking which would provide the background for further explorations.

1. From the discussions I understood that the legal reaffirmation of all the obligations under the Constantinople Convention should not present any difficulty; this is a question of form, not of substance. I further understood that it would not present any difficulties to widen the obligations under the Convention to cover the questions of maximum tolls (as at present); maintenance and development; reporting to the United Nations.

2. Nor should, if I understood the sense of the discussions correctly, the questions of the Canal code and the regulations present any difficulties of substance, as I understood the situation to

be that no revision of the code or the regulations was envisaged which would lead to rules less adequate than the present rules. I further understood that revisions would be subject to consultation.

3. Nor, in my understanding, should the question of tolls and charges present any difficulties, as according to what emerged in the discussions, the manner of fixing tolls and charges would be subject to agreement, as also the reservation of a certain part of the dues for development purposes would be subject to agreement.

4. Nor, in my understanding, should the *principle* of organized co-operation between an Egyptian authority and the users give rise to any differences of views, while, on the other hand, it obviously represents a field where the arrangements to be made call for careful exploration in order to make sure that they would meet the three first requirements approved by the Security Council. The following points in the summing up of my understanding of the sense of the discussions refer to this question of implementation of an organized co-operation:

A. The co-operation requires obviously an organ on the Egyptian side (the authority in charge of the operation of the Canal), and a representation of the users, recognized by the Canal authority (and the Egyptian Government) and entitled to speak for the users.

B. Provisions should be made for joint meetings between the authority and the representation to all the extent necessary to effect the agreed co-operation.

C. Within the framework of the co-operation, the representation should be entitled to raise all matters affecting the users' rights or interests, for discussion and consultation or by way of complaint. The representation should, on the other hand, of course not, in exercising its functions, do this in such a way as to interfere with the administrative functions of the operating organ.

D. The co-operation which would develop on the basis of points A–C would not give satisfaction to the three first requirements approved by the Security Council unless completed with arrangements for fact-finding, reconciliation, recourse to appropriate juridical settlement of possible disputes and guarantees for execution of the results of reconciliation or juridical settlements of disputes.

E. (a) Fact-finding can be provided for by direct access for the party concerned to a checking of relevant facts, or by a standing (joint) organ, with appropriate representation for both parties;

(b) A standing (joint) organ might also be considered for reconciliation;

(c) In case of unresolved differences, as facts or other relevant questions, not resolved by the arrangements so far mentioned, recourse should be possible—as the case may be—to a standing local organ for arbitration, set up in accordance with common practices, *or* to whatever other arbitration organ found necessary in the light of a further study of the character of the conflicts that may arise, *or* to the International Court of Justice (whose jurisdiction in this case of course should be mandatory), *or* to the Security Council (or whatever other organ of the United Nations that may be established under the rules of the Charter);

(d) Concerning the implementation of findings by a United Nations organ, normal rules should apply. In respect of the implementation of awards made by a standing organ for arbitration, or by whatever other organ may be established for similar purposes, the parties should undertake to recognize the awards as binding, when rendered, and undertake to carry them out in good faith. In case of a complaint because of alleged non-compliance with an award the same arbitration organ which gave the award should register the fact of non-compliance. Such a 'constatation' would give the complaining party access to all normal forms of redress, but also the right to certain steps in self-protection, the possible scope of which should be subject to an agreement in principle; both sides, thus, in case of a 'constatation', should be entitled to certain limited 'police action', even without recourse to further juridical procedures.

5. It was, finally, my understanding that the question covered by the requirement in point 6 of the Security Council resolution, would not give rise to special difficulties, as the subject seems fairly well covered by the formulation of the principle itself.

Whether or not a set of arrangements will meet the three first requirements approved by the Security Council, will, according to my understanding of the situation, depend on the reply to the questions under point 4 above. That is true not only with an arrangement starting from the assumption of operation of the Canal by an Egyptian authority, but also on the assumption that the operation of the Canal (in the narrow sense of the word) is organized in another way. If I have rightly interpreted the sense of the discussions as concerns specifically the questions of verification, recourse and enforcement (point 4, E) and if, thus, no objection in principle is made *a priori* against arrangements as set down above, I would, from a legal and technical point of view—without raising here the political considerations which come into play—consider the framework sufficiently wide to make a further exploration of a possible basis for negotiations along the lines indicated worth trying.

I am sure you appreciate that whatever clarification you may give of your reaction to this interpretation of mine of the possibilities would be helpful for me in contacts with the other parties —of the reactions of which I likewise need a more complete picture—and might smooth the way to progress beyond the point reached in the private talks.

(*Signed*) DAG HAMMARSKJOLD
Secretary-General of the United Nations

8. *Excerpts from Two Cables from Eden to Eisenhower (30 October 1956)*
(*from Eden, pp. 586–7; note and ellipsis in source*)

I

We have never made any secret of our belief that justice entitled us to defend our vital interests against Nasser's designs. But we acted with you in summoning the London Conference, in despatching the abortive Menzies mission and in seeking to establish S.C.U.A.* As you know, the Russians regarded the Security Council proceedings as a victory for themselves and Egypt. Nevertheless we continued through the Secretary-General of the United Nations to seek a basis for the continuation of the negotiations.

Egypt has to a large extent brought this attack on herself by insisting that the state of war persists, by defying the Security Council and by declaring her intention to marshal the Arab states for the destruction of Israel. The latest example of Egyptian intentions is the announcement of a joint command between Egypt, Jordan and Syria.

We have earnestly deliberated what we should do in this serious situation. We cannot afford to see the canal closed or to lose the shipping which is daily on passage through it. We have a responsibility for the people in these ships. We feel that decisive action

* Suez Canal Users' Association.

should be taken at once to stop hostilities. We have agreed with you to go to the Security Council and instructions are being sent this moment. Experience however shows that its procedure is unlikely to be either rapid or effective.

II

Message sent after British talks with the French Ministers and the delivery of their jointly agreed upon notes to the Egyptian Ambassador and the Israeli Chargé d'Affaires.

My first instinct would have been to ask you to associate yourself and your country with the declaration. But I know the constitutional and other difficulties in which you are placed. I think there is a chance that both sides will accept. In any case it would help this result very much if you found it possible to support what we have done at least in general terms. We are well aware that no real settlement of Middle East problems is possible except through the closest co-operation between our two countries. Our two Governments have tried with the best will in the world all sorts of public and private negotiations through the last two or three years and they have all failed. This seems an opportunity for a fresh start.

... Nothing could have prevented this volcano from erupting somewhere, but when the dust settles there may well be a chance for our doing a really constructive piece of work together and thereby strengthening the weakest point in the line against communism.

9. Letter from Eisenhower to Eden (30 October 1956)
(from Eisenhower, pp. 678–9)

Dear Anthony:
I address you in this note not only as head of Her Majesty's Government but as my long-time friend who has, with me, believed in and worked for real Anglo-American understanding.
Last night I invited Mr. Coulson, currently your Washington representative to come to my house to talk over the worsening situation in the Mid East. I have no doubt that the gist of our conversation has already been communicated to you. But it seemed to me desirable that I should give you my impressions concerning

certain phases of this whole affair that are disturbing me very much.

Without bothering here to discuss the military movements themselves and their possible grave consequences, I should like to ask your help in clearing up my understanding as to exactly what is happening between us and our European allies—especially between us, the French and yourselves.

We have learned that the French had provided Israel with a considerable amount of equipment, including airplanes, in excess of the amounts of which we were officially informed. This action was, as you know, in violation of agreements now existing between our three countries. We know also that this process has continued in other items of equipment.

Quite naturally we began watching with increased interest the affairs in the Eastern Mediterranean. Late last week we became convinced that the Israel mobilization was proceeding to a point where something more than mere defense was contemplated, and found the situation serious enough to send a precautionary note to Ben-Gurion. On Sunday we repeated this note of caution and made a public statement of our actions, informing both you and the French of our concern. On that day we discovered that the volume of communication traffic between Paris and Tel Aviv jumped enormously, alerting us to the probability that France and Israel were concerting detailed plans of some kind.

When on Monday actual military moves began, we quickly decided that the matter had to go immediately to the United Nations, in view of our Agreement of May, 1950, subscribed to by our three governments.

Last evening our Ambassador to the United Nations met with your Ambassador, Pierson Dixon, to request him to join us in presenting the case to the United Nations this morning. We were astonished to find that he was completely unsympathetic, stating frankly that his government would not agree to any action whatsoever to be taken against Israel. He further argued that the tripartite statement of May, 1950, was ancient history and without current validity.

Without arguing the point as to whether or not the tri-partite statement is or should be outmoded, I feel very seriously that whenever any agreement or pact of this kind is in spirit renounced by one of its signatories, it is only fair that the other signatories should be notified. Since the United States has continued to look

upon that statement as representing the policies and determination of our three governments, I have not only publicly
announced several times that it represents our policy, but many of
our actions in the Mid East have been based upon it. For example,
we have in the past denied arms both to Egypt and to Israel on the
ground that the 1950 statement was their surest guarantee of
national security. We have had no thought of repudiating that
statement and we have none now.

All this development, with its possible consequences, including
the possible involvement of you and the French in a general
Arab war, seems to me to leave your government and ours in a
very sad state of confusion, so far as any possibility of unified
understanding and action are concerned. It is true that Egypt has
not yet formally asked this government for aid. But the fact is that
if the United Nations finds Israel to be an aggressor, Egypt could
very well ask the Soviets for help—and then the Mid East fat
would really be in the fire. It is this latter possibility that has led
us to insist that the West must ask for a United Nations examin-
ation and possible intervention, for we may shortly find ourselves
not only at odds concerning what we should do, but confronted
with a de facto situation that would make all our present troubles
look puny indeed.

Because of all these possibilities, it seems to me of first importance that the UK and the US quickly and clearly lay out their
present views and intentions before each other, and that, come
what may, we find some way of concerting our ideas and plans so
that we may not, in any real crisis, be powerless to act in concert
because of misunderstanding of each other. I think it is important that our two peoples, as well as the French, have this clear
understanding of our common or several viewpoints.

With warm personal regard.

As ever,
Ike E.

10. Declaration by Government of Egypt (24 April 1957)
(from U.N. Doc. A/3576/S/3818)

In elaboration of the principles set forth in their memorandum
dated 18 [17] March 1957, the Government of the Republic of
Egypt, in accord with the Constantinople Convention of 1888 and

the Charter of the United Nations, make hereby the following Declaration on the Suez Canal and the arrangements for its operation.

1. *Reaffirmation of Convention*

It remains the unaltered policy and firm purpose of the Government of Egypt to respect the terms and the spirit of the Constantinople Convention of 1888 and the rights and obligations arising therefrom. The Government of Egypt will continue to respect, observe and implement them.

2. *Observance of the Convention and of the Charter of the United Nations*

While reaffirming their determination to respect the terms and the spirit of the Constantinople Convention of 1888 and to abide by the Charter and the principles and purposes of the United Nations, the Government of Egypt are confident that the other signatories of the said Convention and all others concerned will be guided by the same resolve.

3. *Freedom of navigation, tolls, and development of the Canal*

The Government of Egypt are more particularly determined:

(a) To afford and maintain free and uninterrupted navigation for all nations within the limits of and in accordance with the provisions of the Constantinople Convention of 1888;

(b) That tolls shall continue to be levied in accordance with the last agreement, concluded on 28 April 1936, between the Government of Egypt and the Suez Canal Maritime Company, and that any increase in the current rate of tolls within any twelve months, if it takes place, shall be limited to 1 percent, any increase beyond that level to be the result of negotiations, and failing agreement, be settled by arbitration according to the procedures set forth in paragraph 7 (b).

(c) That the Canal is maintained and developed in accordance with the progressive requirements of modern navigation and that such maintenance and development shall include the 8th and 9th Programmes of the Suez Canal Maritime Company with such improvements to them as are considered necessary.

4. *Operation and management*

The Canal will be operated and managed by the autonomous

Suez Canal authority established by the Government of Egypt on 26 July 1956. The Government of Egypt are looking forward with confidence to continued co-operation with the nations of the world in advancing the usefulness of the Canal. To that end the Government of Egypt would welcome and encourage co-operation between the Suez Canal Authority and representatives of shipping and trade.

5. *Financial arrangements*

(a) Tolls shall be payable in advance to the account of the Suez Canal Authority at any bank as may be authorized by it. In pursuance of this, the Suez Canal Authority has authorized the National Bank of Egypt and is negotiating with the Bank of International Settlement to accept on its behalf payment of the Canal tolls.

(b) The Suez Canal Authority shall pay to the Government of Egypt 5 percent of all the gross receipts as royalty.

(c) The Suez Canal Authority will establish a Suez Canal Capital and Development Fund into which shall be paid 25 percent of all gross receipts. This Fund will assure that there shall be available to the Suez Canal Authority adequate resources to meet the needs of development and capital expenditure for the fulfilment of the responsibilities they have assumed and are fully determined to discharge.

6. *Canal Code*

The regulations governing the Canal, including the details of its operation, are embodied in the Canal Code which is the law of the Canal. Due notice will be given of any alteration in the Code, and any such alteration, if it affects the principles and commitments in this Declaration and is challenged or complained against for that reason, shall be dealt with in accordance with the procedures set forth in paragraph 7 (b).

7. *Discrimination and complaints relating to the Canal Code*

(a) In pursuance of the principles laid down in the Constantinople Convention of 1888, the Suez Canal Authority, by the terms of its Charter, can in no case grant any vessel, company or other party any advantage or favour not accorded to other vessels, companies or parties on the same conditions.

(b) Complaints of discrimination or violation of the Canal Code shall be sought to be resolved by the complaining party by reference to the Suez Canal Authority. In the event that such a reference does not resolve the complaint, the matter may be referred, at the option of the complaining party or the Authority, to an arbitration tribunal composed of one nominee of the complaining party, one of the Authority and a third to be chosen by both. In case of disagreement, such third member will be chosen by the President of the International Court of Justice upon the application of either party.

(c) The decisions of the arbitration tribunal shall be made by a majority of its members. The decisions shall be binding upon the parties when they are rendered and they must be carried out in good faith.

(d) The Government of Egypt will study further appropriate arrangements that could be made for fact-finding, consultation and arbitration on complaints relating to the Canal Code.

8. Compensation and claims

The question of compensation and claims in connexion with the nationalization of the Suez Canal Maritime Company shall, unless agreed between the parties concerned, be referred to arbitration in accordance with the established practice.

9. Disputes, disagreements or differences arising out of the Convention and this Declaration

(a) Disputes or disagreements arising in respect of the Constantinople Convention of 1888 or this Declaration shall be settled in accordance with the Charter of the United Nations.

(b) Differences arising between the parties to the said Convention in respect of the interpretation or the applicability of its provisions, if not otherwise resolved, will be referred to the International Court of Justice. The Government of Egypt would take the necessary steps in order to accept the compulsory jurisdiction of the International Court of Justice in conformity with the provisions of Article 36 of its Statute.

10. Status of this Declaration

The Government of Egypt make this Declaration, which reaffirms and is in full accord with the terms and spirit of the Constantinople Convention of 1888, as an expression of their desire and determination to enable the Suez Canal to be an efficient and adequate waterway linking the nations of the world and serving the cause of peace and prosperity.

This Declaration with the obligations therein, constitutes an international instrument and will be deposited and registered with the Secretariat of the United Nations.

2. COMMENT

STEPHEN M. SCHWEBEL

Professor Bowie's analysis of the roles of law in the Suez crisis of 1956 indicates the multiplicity of those roles and the varying applications of them. A few further comments may be in order.

1. The United States was not alone in its actual and professed attachment to norms of the United Nations Charter, notably to the fundamental prescription of Article 2, paragraph 4 that States shall refrain in their international relations from the threat or use of force against the territorial integrity or political independence of other States. Most members of the General Assembly backed the United States and Secretary-General Dag Hammarskjold. To be sure, that majority may have been essentially animated by its political opposition to the Suez invasion. But it was undoubtedly sensitive to the fact that the central legal norms of the Charter were at stake.

Suez was not of course the first time when those norms had been challenged. They had been challenged by indirect Communist aggression against Greece in the earliest days of the organization's life; by the invasion by the Arab States of what was Palestine and what became Israel in 1948; and by the attack upon the Republic of Korea in 1950. And, at the very hour of Suez in 1956, Hungary was subjected to brutal Soviet aggression, which yielded not an iota to the condemnation of the United Nations.

Thus what was remarkable in the eyes of the United Nations majority was not so much the singular character of this violation of the Charter as the character of the principal violators, Great Britain and France. Britain, with the United States, had been the founder of the League of Nations; with France, she had been its main (if uncertain) power; and, with the United States, it was Britain which was a principal source and support of the United Nations. Great Britain and France enjoyed great traditions as pillars of international law and creators of international institutions; and they were and remain great democratic States.

It accordingly was shocking to enlightened international public opinion that Great Britain and France should employ force in open violation of Charter principles. I well remember hearing the late James T. Shotwell emotionally describe the day and night he spent at the General Assembly amidst condemnations of Britain and France 'as the saddest day of my life', by which, I think, he meant that States which to him had been the primary upholders of international law and order since the Versailles Conference had betrayed their tradition. Dag Hammarskjold too did not conceal his pain; the Anglo-French action mocked behind-the-scenes negotiations in the Security Council. And he, like many Members of the General Assembly, was moved by the feeling that, if Britain and France could not be brought to support Charter principles, those principles were in mortal danger, for the future of international organization, as had its past, significantly lay in the hands of the great democracies.

In this sense, the uses of international law are discriminatory; the relatively responsible and relatively democratic States are expected to adhere to international law more regularly and more profoundly than other States. The General Assembly expects more, and gets more, from them than it does from authoritarian States, most notably the Communist Members. It is assumed that international law will more significantly condition the behaviour of the West; tools which may work are applied with energy. But the General Assembly majority shows less inclination to endeavour to hold either itself or its less continent Members to international standards. It is not only the Communist States that benefit by what is in fact a double standard: so do the countries of the 'Third World'. Aggression by Syria against Jordan and Lebanon; unlawful intervention by Egypt and Libya in the affairs of other States; genocidal behaviour in Burundi and Bengal—this and much more does not gain the attention, still less the condemnation, of the United Nations. In part, this may be because the Soviet Union for years has vetoed (as in the case of aggression by Sukarno's Indonesia against Malaysia) any action in the Security Council unacceptable to its favourites among the 'unaligned' States. The Council can accordingly be no more depended upon for relatively objective decisions than can the General Assembly.

The discriminatory application of international law is not a new phenomenon. But it may have entered a new stage of acuity in the last ten or fifteen years, stemming in part perhaps from the influx of new States into the General Assembly and their susceptibility to bloc voting. The phenomenon is especially visible in international organs. In the ordinary run of bilateral relations between States, the traditional and essential reciprocity of international law has wider play.

2. The United States is of course not free of the tendency to apply international law more rigorously to the conduct of others than to that of itself. It may be said that the Suez case is illustrative. Eisenhower and Dulles appear to have been genuine in their perception of the Anglo-French action as a violation of Charter principles. But it may be wondered if they paused to give similar consideration to the reputed activities of the Central Intelligence Agency a few years before in the overthrow of the Mossadegh Government in Iran and the Arbenz Government in Guatemala. It may be that what is reputed is not factual; the United States may not have played the role attributed to the C.I.A. Or it may be that Eisenhower and Dulles made some distinction between well-concealed and badly concealed efforts to overthrow offensive governments. If the latter is the case, such a distinction would obviously have no legal force; the equipping and training of Guatemalan opponents of the Arbenz Government would be as much an illustration of indirect aggression as the Anglo-French attack at Suez was one of direct aggression. Doubts about American behaviour in instances such as these raise doubts about the objectivity of the Eisenhower–Dulles approach in the Suez affair. And events after Suez demonstrate that the United States was no more disposed to respect Charter principles when it saw its vital interests to be in conflict with them than were Britain and France in 1956. Quite apart from U.S. behaviour in other instances before and after Suez, in that very case Dulles seems to have admitted the threat of applying force even if debarring its use, a threat no less unlawful under the regime of the United Nations Charter.

But the uneven application and irregular effectiveness of international law hardly shows that it does not act as one moulder of and constraint upon State conduct. In some cases, its impact may be much greater than others; but in any event, international law in multiple ways influences and is influenced by the unfolding facts of international life.

INDEX

27, 102–3; divergence from U.S., 15, 28, 35–6, 42–7, 61, 65, 102–3; need for U.S. support, 23, 103; policy in Suez dispute, 25–8, 103, 107; view of Nasser, 26–8; collusion with British and Israelis, 30–1, 51, 52, 53–60, 108; at Tripartite talks, 36–7; and Eighteen-Power Proposal, 40, 42; view of S.C.U.A., 44–7; appeal to U.N. Security Council, 47–52, 107–8; ultimatum to Israel and Egypt, 59, 60, 66; action in Security Council, October 1956, 62, 67, 68; military action against Egypt, 68, 70, 73–7; and U.N.E.F., 73; troop withdrawal, 78–9, 82–5; use of law and legal means, 102–3, 104, 107–8, 109. *See also* Algeria

Gaitskell, Hugh, 20, 24, 25, 44–5, 75
Gaza Raid, 10, 54
Gaza Strip: Egyptian bases in, 56, 60; U.N.E.F. operations, 75, 92–3, 94, 95, 96; issue of, for Israel, 86, 87, 89, 90, 109, 110; Israeli withdrawal from, 92, 95; Egyptian governor for, 95–6
Glubb, Lieut.-Gen. Sir John Bagot, 11–12, 18, 19

Hammarskjold, Dag: and Security Council private talks, 49–50; letter to Fawzi, 50–1, 129–32; and Anglo-French military action, 68–9, 76, 82; concept of Secretary-General, 69, 111–12; and formation of U.N.E.F., 71–3, 74–7, 111; and entry and operation of U.N.E.F., 78–85, 92, 112; and Anglo-French troop withdrawal, 83; Canal clearance, 83–4; and Israeli withdrawal, 87–94, 109, 110; on Egyptian rights in Gaza, 96; and new Egyptian regime for Canal, 96–7; conception of law, 112; attitude towards political settlement, 113
Hitler, 20, 26, 28, 31, 32, 43, 51
Hungary, 59, 62, 63, 76, 101, 115
Hussein ibn Talal, King of Jordan, 11, 19

Imperialism, 1, 2, 30, 32, 45, 62, 67
India: and London Conference, 36 n., 38, 39, 40; attitude towards Nasser, 48; in General Assembly, 69, 83; and U.N.E.F., 72
International Bank for Reconstruction

and Development (I.B.R.D.), 11, 12
International Court of Justice, 92, 97
Iran, 9, 29–30, 36 n., 40, 58, 94
Israel: and arms supply to Middle East, 9, 11; Gaza Raid, 10, 54; shipping barred, 5, 17, 20, 23 n., 28, 38, 54–5, 56, 66, 89–90, 92–3, 96, 97, 104, 109–10; French military aid to, 27, 55; British and French collusion with, 51, 52, 53–60, 104, 108; hostility to Nasser, 54; raid against Jordan, 58; attack on Egypt, 60, 66; Anglo-French ultimatum, 60, 66; resentment against U.S., 65; justification of force, 66–7; troop withdrawal, 83, 85–96; use of law, 103–4, 108–10; issue of political settlement, 113–14; Six Day War, 113–14

Jordan, 11, 58–9, 60

Labour Party (British), 20, 24–5, 53, 57, 75, 103
Lacoste, Robert, 26
Law: Nasser's position, 16–17, 110–11; Anglo-French views, 23–4, 27, 28, 67, 102–3, 107–8, 109; opinions of the Lord Chancellor and Lord McNair, 24; U.S. use of, 33–4, 99–100, 102, 104–8, 115; and blockades, 54–5, 92–3, 110; Israeli use of, 66–7, 85, 89, 103–4, 108–10; Egyptian rights in Gaza, 95–6; use by parties, in general, 99–104, in first phase, 104–8, after resort to force, 108–11; crisis impact on instruments of, 111–14; role of, appraised, 114–15
Lebanon, 38, 94, 99
Less developed nations, 39–40, 62
Lloyd, Selwyn, 44, 49–51, 59, 83, 84, 107–8
Lodge, Henry Cabot, 72, 94, 95
London Conference, 14, 16, 36, 54, 100, 101, 106; proceedings, 38–40, 41. *See also* Second London Conference

Macmillan, Harold: view of crisis, 20–1, 22; and Robert Murphy, 22, 31; and Eighteen-Power Proposal, 40; on Canal operation by Egypt, 51; and political misjudgement, 58; on Britain's economic straits, 64
Malta, 22, 108
Meir, Mrs. Golda, 87, 95
Menzies, Sir Robert, 16, 40–2, 43, 54, 107

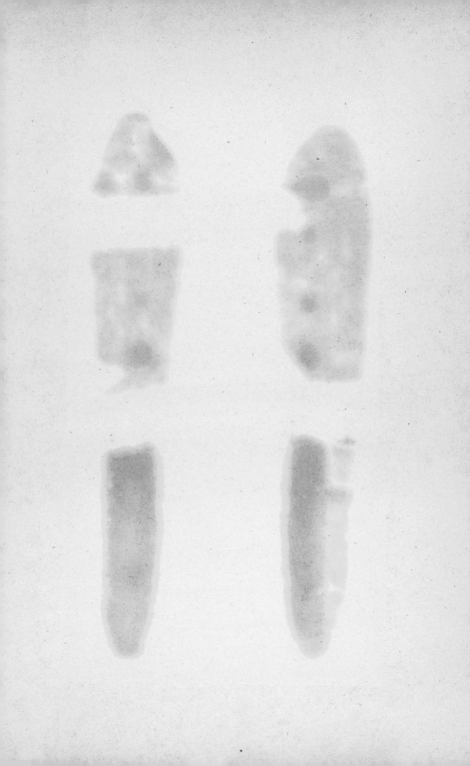

75290

BOWIE, ROBERT
    SUEZ 1956.

DATE DUE

GAYLORD   PRINTED IN U.S.A.